POWER OF THE PAUSE

WHEN A *Female Executive* CAN NO LONGER HIDE BEHIND HIGH-FUNCTIONING ANXIETY AND DEPRESSION

DR. EBONY STONE

SOUTHFIELD, MI

THE POWER OF THE PAUSE:

When a female executive can longer hide behind high-functioning anxiety and depression

The information in this book is based on the author's knowledge, experience, and opinions. The ideas and methods described in this book are not intended to be a definitive set of instructions. You may discover other methods and materials to accomplish the same end result. Your results may differ.

PUBLISHED BY: Black Woman in the Corner Office, LLC

To request permissions, please contact the publisher at:

BLACK WOMAN IN THE CORNER OFFICE, LLC

info@drebonystone.com

Paperback ISBN: 979-8-218-40069-9

First Paperback Edition: May 2024

Edited by: Khloe's Thoughts Editing

Cover by: Make Your Mark Publishing Solutions

Layout by: Make Your Mark Publishing Solutions

CONTENTS

ACKNOWLEDGMENTS

Thank you to my husband, Quadir. Your unwavering belief in my abilities, your unconditional love, and your example of faith in action for our family means everything to me. I could not have done this without you. Even when I doubted myself, you reminded me of who and whose I am.

Thank you to my children, Yatil, Niya, and Emory. For most of your life you have had to share your mom with the world as everyone tugged on me for something, but you did it graciously and have grown into amazing young adults that I am immensely proud of.

Thank you to my mom for being the very best mom anyone could ask for. I know I was a doozy to deal with growing up, but you kept me in check, and I am forever grateful. None of this would have been possible without your love and support.

To my brother—my very first best friend—Thanks for it all!

To the rest of my family, friends, and support system, thank you for being the most amazing encouragers a girl could have.

Lastly, to my therapist—thank you for helping me be courageous enough to tell my story in hopes that it helps someone else.

"I can do all things, through Christ, who strengthens me."
–Philippians 4:13 NKJV

DEDICATION

This book is dedicated to my daddy…I did it, Daddy… miss you old man!

For I know the plans I have for you," says the Lord, "They are plans for good and not for disaster, to give you a future and a hope."

—Jeremiah 29:11, NLT

PREFACE

If you don't know me, you might ask, "who is she anyway?" or "why is she writing a book?" or better yet, "why should I read it?" Well, let me take a stab at explaining it by sharing some of the things you might see in a bio or hear in an introduction of me for a speaking engagement. Ebony Stone is a devout Christian, not afraid to let anyone and everyone know that her faith is important to her and something she continues to nurture. She is the loyal wife of a gentleman that she says still gives her butterflies after twenty-two years of marriage and a mother to three of the absolutely most wonderful human beings to walk this earth— you will see more of each of them as they take this world by storm in their own ways, that she is sure of. When it comes to being a wife and mother, she's often been quoted saying, "please don't ever make me choose between anything and my family because I can tell you in advance, my family will win every time." She is a dedicated daughter to a father that watches over her from heaven, a mother that still cooks her meals often, and a mother-in-love that she bowls with weekly. She is the passionate older sister to two brothers (and a sister who passed away years ago). She is "momtie" aunt to four nieces (one who passed away far too soon) and two nephews. She is the niece and cousin to many. She is a friend that can be counted on to be there when you need her whether it is to just laugh with you about the antics of your early years or to tell you when you are on the wrong side of an argument. She is a pillar in the community, donating time and money to causes that help our people. She is an accomplished executive that climbed the corporate ladder unscathed with a tremendous reputation for creating strategy and building teams that produce results. She is an educated woman holding three degrees including the terminal degree of DBA that allows her to adorn the title of doctor. She is an entrepreneur constantly looking for ways to leave wealth and legacy to future generations of her family. However, if you ask her, she'll tell you, "At my heart, I am just a girl from the west side of Detroit, trying to make a small difference in my own little way."

Yep, that's right ... that's all true. That's me.
I am a woman.
I am a Christian woman.
I am a Black Christian woman.
I am a Black, educated Christian woman.
I am a Black, educated, Christian female executive.
I am a Black, educated, Christian, female executive in a competitive industry.
I am a Black, educated, Christian, wife, mother, daughter, sister, aunt, niece, cousin, and friend that just happens to be an executive, a strategist, a coach, a mentor, a lifelong learner and student, a board member, an entrepreneur, and writer, etc.
I am every woman.

But that is the problem, I am NOT every woman. I am just one woman. While I love the characters and the actors that played them on TV and even dreamed of walking, talking, dressing, owning, and accomplishing things like they accomplished, I am not the fictional characters I often watched on television. I am not Clair Huxtable; I am not the always put together attorney with five kids married to the doctor and being the mom of the ideal nuclear family. I am not Olivia Pope; I am not the style icon, high profile fixer, leading a team of gladiators. I am not Jessica Pearson; I am not the named partner of a prestigious law firm ultimately taking the fall so that her team can continue to flourish. I am not Joan Clayton; I am not the sometimes-quirky attorney with the high-powered best friend realtor who is looking for love while always trying to be the supportive friend. I am not Analise Keating; I am not the college professor with the deep wounds trying her best to help students through the mess of drama that accompanies her life. I am not any of those women. Those are fictional characters that I love, that we all love. They are examples of the power and complexity of the Black woman, but they are not real. I see a bit of myself in each of those characters, but I am not them. I am powerful, I am complex, and I am a Black woman, but I am not every woman.

While I love the real-life Black woman superheroes that plaster our billboards and social media feeds, I am not them. I am not Michelle Obama; I haven't a clue (nor do any of us) what it must be like to be the wife of our first Black president and raise a family in that limelight. I am not Oprah Winfrey; I don't have billions or own a media empire. I am not Beyonce; I don't have a beehive ready to sting at the first insult anyone sends my way. I am not Kamala Harris; I am not the first Black woman to be vice president of the United States—I am not aware of being the first Black woman to do anything. I am not Sarah Jakes Roberts;

I am not the daughter of a mega preacher getting on stages and delivering powerful sermons that transform the lives of millions. They are real life examples of the power the Black woman yields. I love them all, and I see a bit of myself in each of them, but I am not them.

While I love the unrequited heroes of my life that many of you will never get the chance to know, I am not Linda Brown (my mother), the hard working, perfect example of sacrificing for your family, disciplinarian that taught us why tough love is important and beat cancer's ass twice by showing us what faith in action really looks like. I am not my daughter, the sassy, talented gifted millennial that is traveling a path new and scary to me for a young adult but proving to the world it doesn't have to be their way; she can do it a new way with God's help. I am not Willie Lee or Bessie Lee (my grandmothers) that put their hearts into every dish they ever made to the point you could taste it, had a green thumb that rivaled that of the master gardeners we learn from today, and raised families on little to nothing monetarily, but with a whole lot of Jesus and a whole lot of love. I am not my aunts, each different in their own way, but making a mark on the family that is unforgettable. I am not my mother-in-love, the entrepreneur with the melodic voice that is giving almost to a fault, that fights ailments in way that proves not her strength, but God's strength. I am not my cousins, I am not my friends, I am not my co-workers, peers, or anyone else. I am just me, the uniquely designed, quirky, eccentric, intelligent woman God made me to be—just as each of you reading this book are uniquely designed to be what God intends for you to be.

I don't know about you, but for me, I know it is time to take off the cape. It is time for me to stop chasing the dream that the world has for me and their plan for me and it is time to chase the purpose that God has for me through the dreams he has placed inside of me. It is time to stop carrying the weight of the world on my shoulders. It is time to stop censoring the game. It is time to stop trying to be everything to everybody. It is time to just be me. It is time to just be you. It's time to pause, to realize the power in the pause.

It was not easy for me to recognize the need for the pause in my life. In fact, I did not recognize the need. The signs for me to stop the unrealistic perfectionism that existed within— the need to stop the extreme pace at which I was running—were all there. The signs were there in massive neon blinking lights that I'd ignored for far too long. I will be eternally grateful for the people in my life that pointed out the signs and made me take a much-needed detour to pause! This is the story of how I came to realize the need to pause and *The Power of the Pause*.

Chapter One

SHE VS. ME

I'll never forget it. I was sitting in what had become my safe space, my car. I often parked it back by my garage with the windows down facing my vegetable garden and pointed at my back yard, the point where four yards came together, and I could watch my neighbors' kids laugh and play on the playscape with not a care in the world. My vegetable garden had become a hobby during the height of the pandemic that gave me escape from what seemed like a never-ending onslaught of challenges. The garden reminded me of the goodness of God and all his majesty. Watching a seed turn into a plant, and arranging the plants in such a way that they created beautiful scenery had in some ways become cleansing to me. I could literally spend hours getting lost in planting, pruning, weeding, and harvesting. But today, this view served as the backdrop for what would be the first day of a shift in the journey of my life. I thought it was just the site of my therapy session, but it would prove to be much more. I'd made the decision to return to therapy because something in my life just wasn't right. I knew I needed help and just didn't know what I needed help with.

To the outside world, I was functioning just fine. Still attaining promotion after promotion, still mentoring and coaching, still being the ultimate professional. Still doing the very best I could to be a great mom and wife. But inside of me, inside was a different story. I carried a sense of sadness that was unexplainable if you've never experienced it. I was cranky, I had crying spells, and my most valued relationships were suffering. I knew something was simply off. I shared my feelings with my physician multiple times and multiple times he suggested therapy or in the medical terminology, multiple times he made a behavioral health referral. I am a big believer in therapy, but this time I was scared of what I might find and how it might change the trajectory of my life and career. I was approaching fifty years old and lots of things for me and my friends were changing on the health spectrum. I wasn't ready for any bad news. After several months, I relented and made a therapy appointment with a therapist I trusted.

I started having my therapy sessions from the car because it was the only place I would not be interrupted. It was the only place that didn't require I empty myself giving to everyone else. It was the only place I could focus on the words of the therapist. It felt like I could actually speak words in that vehicle that I couldn't speak anywhere else, so I started therapy this time from the front seat of the car. I'd been in individual therapy before but left for different reasons. I really can't tell you why I left the first time except that I was young and immature. I was a young adult experiencing some of the same symptoms I was experiencing this time, but I think I believed I was invincible as most young adults do. The second time I left, I was not a big fan of the therapist. I also hadn't learned the value of interviewing and choosing my care professionals to make sure they were right for me. The next time it took me a while to make the time to find the right therapist. The third time, I left really hurt. I loved the therapist. She really got me and I was making progress, but when I walked out into the waiting room and saw someone that would eventually become one of the "mean girls" in my life awaiting her appointment with the same therapist, I didn't return. This time I was determined that things would be different, I would get what I needed and I would stay in therapy no matter what.

This time, I was much more intentional about what I wanted to accomplish in therapy and about my choice of a therapist. I chose a Black woman as my therapist because I simply wanted some things to be understood. Living in this world as a Black woman is something that only a Black woman could understand. My boss couldn't understand, most of my peers couldn't understand, most of those that worked for me couldn't understand. It was not something that I wanted to spend hours and dollars trying to explain. I just wanted it to be understood. I chose a Christian therapist for the same reason. I didn't want to have to explain my faith, I wanted it to be understood and a part of the therapy process. I chose someone outside of the network of my employer's health care system because I simply didn't trust that my experience would be confidential. I trusted the health care providers. What I didn't trust was who might have access to the records and access them. I was intentional, deliberate, determined, and enjoyed my therapy sessions.

It was only a few weeks of my weekly sessions before she mentioned wanting to do a few evaluations. It took me several weeks to get through the two evaluations. When the results of the evaluations were back, my therapist delivered the results in the caring and tender way she always spoke. I knew I was stressed, and a bit anxious, but Major Depressive Disorder and High Functioning Anxiety were the furthest things from my mind. She was pleasant and very "therapist like" in her delivery, but for me the words rang out with such viciousness the only word I can think of to describe the feeling is stinging. It was as if the words themselves were akin to thousands of bees attacking me. I'd been feeling like everything I'd touched lately turned to shit, this was yet another thing.

I mean, my physician had already tried a couple medications to try to help me sleep, as I'd not been sleeping well for a year or a bit longer. The medications didn't work, or worked so well I was walking around like a zombie for days. I was going to therapy for a reason. I had suspicions that I was experiencing something that required a diagnosis. My therapist had already told me what she was assessing me for, but I wasn't ready to hear it. It had taken me multiple sessions to just get through the first assessment, and then another couple of sessions for the second. I didn't know why the words felt like daggers when I finally had to hear them but they did. In some way, I felt excruciating pain and numbness at the same time. There was also part of me that felt relief. I didn't know why the emotions I had were whirling around like someone had put my feelings in a snow globe and shook them up. Well, that's not true, I did know why they felt that way. My emotions being all over the place made me feel weak, like I was not strong enough to handle life while everyone else was handling life like a breeze, or so it seemed. They made me feel like an imposter. *How had I mentored and coached so many people through extremely difficult scenarios, if this was my truth? These emotions made me feel like a failure. How could I experience this and still be considered a professional that had things under control? I'm supposed to have this all together. I'm that girl! I'd fought so hard to get here, to overcome the mistakes of my past, to push forward to be all that I could be. How could this be my reality?* The interesting thing was that the words of the therapist also made me feel like a victor. They helped me to finally feel like I was at the turning point of a losing race when the underdog overtakes the leader by just an inch, and you can see the determination on their face and know they will end up victorious. There was so much happening, so many emotions, so many contradictions whirling inside of me.

"Mrs. Stone," the therapist said, "you have a severe anxiety disorder and you are suffering from severe depression."

I just looked at her on the screen. I was processing the words but processing them slowly. I wanted to fight the tears, but I wanted to let them go all at the same time. I finally stopped fighting the tears. I stopped trying to hold back. The fight in me disappeared and tears started running down my face. That was the only response I could muster. I couldn't fight any longer. *Or had the fight just begun by letting the tears run?*

"Take your time and process it, I know it's difficult to hear," the therapist continued, "with this diagnosis, I am recommending you be removed from work for a minimum of 4 to 6 weeks, at that point we will reassess and determine next steps."

The only audible response I could come up with was..."okay."

"Take some time and sit with this and then you let me know when you want the leave to start. Your brain needs a hard reset. You've been operating in a deficit for so long, you don't even realize that is what you are doing. We can start your leave as early as tomorrow," the therapist politely communicated.

Time off of work, great right? Why was this stinging so badly? Why was I crying so hard? Who couldn't use a break? Why were all the previously mentioned thoughts there? They were true...weren't they? What was happening? Could I recover?

Finally, She came out. She...the always professional, always on point, always working toward a goal, always making the family proud, always an example for other Black women, always an example for anyone really, always controlling her words as not to offend, always figuring out the difficult stuff, always making balancing it all look easy, always cheering on and celebrating others, always appearing to be okay on the outside. The alter ego. My professional Sasha Fierce, the one that was definitely part of me, definitely real, but not all of me. She showed up...

"Well, I'd like to talk to my physician first and get his thoughts. I have an appointment with him on Tuesday anyway. I can talk to him then," She said.

She had found a way to try to take control of this situation and stand strong, say and do "the right thing" because that is what She does.

The therapist responded ever so gently. "Okay. You see him and I will schedule our next session after you see him so we can make some final decisions. I know how you feel about medication. I want you to know that when you give him this report, he is going to suggest medication."

Medication, what the entire hell!! I'm just tired. I don't need another fucking pill, I just need a vacation and I'll be fine.

But, of course, those thoughts couldn't be uttered in words, they weren't acceptable, She had learned that the world couldn't handle her real thoughts so She said, "That's fair. He [my primary care physician] knows how I feel about medication, I'll hear him out but the likelihood of me taking medication for this is low."

Sure as shit, when I saw him he suggested medication. I'd expected that because I was forewarned. What I hadn't expected was his lack of surprise when I told him the diagnosis from the therapist. I was taken back by the nonchalant nature with which he approached the situation. Not because he didn't have any bedside manner, he in fact did; he was an amazingly caring doctor, but he didn't think that I would be surprised by anything he said so he simply communicated bluntly.

"Well yeah, Mrs. Stone, we've known you've been dealing with something for at least a year or so. That is the reason I'd made the behavioral health recommendations months ago. I'm glad you are finally taking steps toward healing. Your mental and emotional health are just as important as your physical health. In some cases, even more, because they can contribute to the decline of your physical health in ways you don't recognize. I'm sure that is some of what you're experiencing now. With your current battle against diabetes and high blood pressure, a continued walk down the road you're on without treatment can be a recipe for disaster. The stress, anxiety, and depression on top of your physical ailments. If left untreated this could lead to heart attack, stroke, or even worse. I agree with your therapist, you MUST take some time off work. I'd like to also explore some medications that can help...blah, blah, blah."

Here we go, another pill. No...Hell No! I thought.

Again, that wasn't the response, though. She said, "well, you know I'd really like to get off the medication I am currently on, so I really don't want to add yet another pill. However, if you prescribe it, I will take it home, read about it, and make a decision from there."

"Okay," he asserted. "I would like for you to strongly consider it. Talk therapy is great but sometimes you need a little more. The medication I am suggesting is not addictive and we will start with low doses, you can then come off of it."

I'd later learn the medical term for starting with small dosing and increasing slowly is titrate, but had he said that to me in that moment, I might have just checked out so I am glad he didn't. He continued, "if it isn't working or you don't like the way it makes you feel we will adjust as necessary. By the way, I'm gonna have the nurse come back and take your blood pressure again, it's really elevated today."

Shit, shit, shit!! Guess I'm not coming off of blood pressure meds any time soon. Don't cry, don't cry, don't cry. You gotta go back across the street to work. You got this.

I really didn't have it, though. I was breaking. Ebony needed to show up in this world more than anything. She could no longer be Ebony's representative. I needed to find the rest of Ebony and let her shine. She had to go, but after decades of letting *She* be in the forefront, I didn't know how to let Ebony out. *How had She become so prominent? Why did it happen? How do I dig up the buried pieces of me to let them shine? Was this life pause the answer?*

She had managed so many things outside of the home, so many different schedules for different extracurriculars for the kids, Sunday date night dancing class, board service, extended family obligations, church, work, a social life, etc. The house always looked like a tornado had gone through it. There were so many things in disrepair that Ebony was embarrassed for all except those closest to her to even come inside. She often explained it away. *It's okay, take a week off next quarter and pull it all together*, she'd say to herself. Next year, next quarter never came and Ebony felt a little more like a failure on the inside each day that she looked at the piles of unwashed laundry, the dishes that didn't get done, the office that showed well on camera but she could barely move around in because of the clutter, the garage that she couldn't park in because of the clutter, the drywall that needed to be repaired in the kitchen, in her dressing area, and in her sons bedroom and bathroom; the doors that needed to be painted; the accent wall in the bedroom that needed to be finished; the faceplates that need to be put on outlets. All those things had been neglected and more. I definitely couldn't decorate the way I wanted to create the retreat-like home feel I'd wanted until some of these things were completed. All of the things that needed to be completed were well within her ability to do, but She had other things that needed to be done so She just let Ebony deal with that as She went on to do the things that the outside world needed to see from her day-to-day life. She had completely taken over.

Chapter Two

VISIBLY INVISIBLE

How did I get here? That is an extremely loaded question. I'll explore some of the things you'd probably expect and some you don't in the coming chapters but let's just look at the last year. The last couple of years had been a freaking roller coaster to say the least. My personal and professional lives had been filled with things to celebrate and things to mourn simultaneously.

There was so much going on in my personal life. My twenty-three-year-old moved back in the house and then out again. My eighteen-year-old experienced her senior year and it was quite tumultuous (momma took that ride with her), then she went off to college across the country. My fifteen-year-old was finally figuring out his way socially at a pretty rigorous school and had found his love of musical instruments (momma was on that ride, too). He'd picked up two new instruments and required more equipment. My husband's business was doing well again after the drought it experienced during the pandemic. Mom's cancer was still in remission, and she was still caring for us all as usual, but I could tell she missed Dad and wanted some companionship. I won't go into any details about their stories, those are theirs to share when and if they want to. Just know that each of them were wild rides and I was on each ride playing the role of the ride or die I'd trained myself to be. *But that was just life, right? Right!* Those things were the things that each of us was bound to run into in this thing we call life. I'd coupled those things with some amazing career moves. To "whom much is given much is required" type career moves.

On top of being alongside each of them, I'd been on my own powerful journey. I'd gotten a promotion to Executive Vice President. It felt great to be recognized for my hard work. She was doing exactly what everyone expected…climbing the ranks. For the first time in my life, I'd sought a promotion when it wasn't even posted, simply by asking for it. I'd not only gotten the initial promotion to Senior Vice President; one I'd been promised in my previous division and then told that a change had been made and the title or increase in salary wouldn't be given because I'd had too many raises in the past couple of years. But after not quite a year in the position, I'd been chosen among some extremely talented and worthy competition to be promoted to Executive Vice President. In order to make these moves, She'd ignored some of her own rules, rules that served her well in the past. Rules that by ignoring contributed to the stress and anxiety she began to feel daily and would eventually lead to full blown disorders.

The organization I was working for was on a wild ride of its own. The organization had gone through workforce reductions in the previous eighteen months and that is a hard pill to swallow. People think it's easy for those that stay or that are in the know.

People figure you've still got your job, so you should be good or think that you've been walking around for months knowing what was coming and just not saying anything, but it is so much different in reality - tougher than people think. There is a tremendous amount of guilt one carries, about how the lives of others are being affected, especially when it happens multiple times and there is no other choice. When people think you are making the calls and you're not, it can wear on you. I simply got to execute on decisions being made at the highest levels, but I didn't really get to make those decisions. I understood the decisions the company had to make and even agreed with the decisions at the core because we just had too many people for the amount of work coming in the door. It just didn't make good business sense to keep such a large staff. That didn't make it easier, though. It was rough. The guilt of being a survivor and getting promotions during that time, although I felt I deserved them, made the experience so much more difficult and guilt riddled for me.

To make matters worse, I no longer enjoyed the work. I loved the people but not the work. I could give two shits about turn times, NPS scores, or any of the innovations we were working on. I'd lost my love for what I did daily, but She knew She had to keep her game face on because jobs that pay like hers and have the benefits her family needed don't come a dime a dozen. Plus, with the youngest attending an elite private school and the middle child at an expensive HBCU, She knew She had to continue to do what She did well. For the first time in a long time, She believed She had to do it for the money, to keep the family running as it typically operated.

In retrospect, She'd been developing and training for this her entire life. She'd learned early on to pretend She was okay and try to ignore her own emotions by burying them. While life as a child was good, and mostly uneventful, it wasn't the easiest. Many would look at my life and wonder why I'd say something like that. I grew up with both of my parents and they worked to provide everything they possibly could for us. I come from a loving family, never missed a meal, always had all of my needs met, never experienced any sort of mental, physical, or emotional abuse that many have struggled with. Yet, somehow, for me it was still not easy.

For a long time, I dealt with guilt from my childhood. Not guilt about anything that happened or didn't happen, but guilt that I didn't look back on my childhood and say it was the best ever. So many people sacrificed and made sure I had so many opportunities, so not feeling immense joy about my childhood made me feel guilty. Let me be clear, my childhood didn't make me sad, but it certainly didn't evoke tremendous amounts of joy. Sure, I had joyous memories and hilarious stories to tell, but deep inside of me something was missing. Not the fault of anyone I grew up with, not the fault of my parents, not the fault of my extended family, not the fault of the city I grew up in or any other factor, it was just the truth of what I'd experienced. In retrospect, I believe I'd dealt with undiagnosed anxiety and depression my entire life and She was created to mask it and manage it. Perhaps this was training for the path and purpose God had for me for the legacy that I am to leave here for the world.

I didn't grow up with a ton of money, but I had both of my parents in the same house my entire upbringing and they loved each other fiercely. My paternal grandmother lived about a mile away and I got to spend a ton of time with her. I remember her cooking daily, having the prettiest house on the block, having house plants that were to die for, having backyard barbecues that were the envy of the neighborhood, and loving on us something serious. I had four of my mom's ten sisters right in the city with us and got to see three of them plus their kids often. We kept the traditions of the annual cider mill trip, family Christmas gift exchange, and traveling to the annual family reunion where my mom's other sisters, five brothers, all of her cousins and their kids would join us. My parents even managed to sacrifice enough to send me to private school for a few years along the way. I would finish my secondary education at an elite college preparatory high school in Detroit.

This all sounds great and don't get me wrong, it was amazing. However, when I think about my childhood, my early young adult life, and my career, I think of the words of U.S. congresswoman, Ayanna Presley, during her interview with Tracee Ellis Ross for the 2022 docuseries, *Hair Tales.* Ms. Presley states, "as Black women we live in the dichotomy of being hyper visualized and invisible at the same time." When I heard her say those words, I sat straight up in my bed in the middle of the night because as usual I wasn't sleeping well and had found something on HULU, Netflix, Prime Video, etc. to fill my time until I dozed off for the three to four hours of nightly sleep since that was about all I was getting at that time. This congresswoman had literally summed up the feeling of my life in just one sentence, in just a few seconds, in what seemed to be a fleeting moment that many would never even get to hear. Ayanna Presley understood.

Ayanna Presley spoke of this dichotomy in the physical sense of the word, and I got that, but for me it was more than just physical. I believed I'd been seen and invisible simultaneously my entire life, physically and in other ways. You see, I was always existing between two extremes. Let me give you some examples:

- Dad's family was the fun loving, partying, fighting, if need be, living on the edge type of family while Mom's family was the proper, church going, rule following, we've got ancestors to make proud type of family.
- I lived in an area full of kids that I always played with but never had neighborhood friends. You won't ever hear the stories of me and a childhood friend that are still in touch because they don't exist.
- Dad and Grandma drank every day until I was about twelve, ran the street numbers, and could string together words that would make sailors blush but then they got saved. I all of a sudden found myself in church several times a week, in highly sought after teen programs, and the daughter of the chairman of the deacon board, and eventually the pastor of his own church.
- I was always great at school and understood how to get A's when I needed to. I promise there is a formula. I graduated toward the bottom of my class because for the first two years of high school I was lost socially and emotionally, and now I know why. I was probably depressed, which manifested itself in a number of bad decisions.
- I was a part of the group voted "class clique" in high school, yet somehow always felt alone.
- I am the girlfriend that everyone comes to talk to help solve their problems, and I work diligently to do so. Yet often I find myself alone when I am at an impasse in my own life and have no one to go

to either because they can't relate or because they have their own problems, and I don't want to bother them with mine.

- I'd often hear things like, "oh my, she has grown into such a gorgeous young woman," while fighting my own self esteem issues.
- I cheer when others win awards, nominate others for awards, but have rarely won an award myself, and experienced something as monumental as attaining a doctorate degree (something only 1% of people in the world do) without so much as a small party in my honor.
- I can get on stage and convey a message to thousands, but I am often unheard in small groups I exist in regularly.

I am the living example, the testimony, the definition of living in constant dichotomies. While my childhood was rather uneventful, there are certain memories that stand out, and I now understand why I had to experience them in order to be on the journey I am on.

So, you might wonder how I got to the place that I created a "She" to speak for me. While I can honestly say I was always authentically Ebony, somehow, I also still felt like I was performing. So, as I did the work, I had to explore my entire experience— starting as a child. I think I started feeling like I needed to perform early on, and She was born. Although I was always surrounded by tons of people and a tremendous amount of love, I often felt alone. For all of my childhood I had one really good friend, my younger brother. Yes, there were people I interacted with at school and in the neighborhood, but I bet you to this day if you found those same people and asked them about me, most wouldn't remember me and if they did remember, it was because I was my brother's sister, my cousin's cousin, or something like that. They won't remember me for me. I know this because I have run into countless numbers of them in my adult life, they don't remember me and sometimes don't even notice me, and I am standing right next to them.

I really struggled with relationships with other Black girls, too, which would eventually turn into a struggle to form strong bonds with other Black women, despite a desire so strong to do so that I was known to go to unreasonable lengths to be a friend without reciprocation. One of the earliest memories I have of this struggle is one that I think fully paints the picture of what my experience trying to build strong relationships with other Black women has been like.

No matter what I do, I put my whole heart into it, including playing as a child. When I was about eleven there was a new girl that moved on to our block. Her name was Anitra. Anitra rallied the troops—Leslie from the corner and Sandy from right next door to her. I lived across the street. I was a couple of years younger than Anitra but from what I remember she acted our age. The other two girls were a year or two younger than me. I was often in the same grade as the older siblings of my playmates because I'd been double promoted, but related to those my age, which posed an interesting dynamic in my life and may have been why it was difficult for me to make friends in school.

My parents were good friends with all of their parents so periodically I was allowed to cross the street and play with them.

The summer was going well, and for the first time, I was actually playing with the other girls on my block. *I might really be making friends.* I woke up daily, went to Grandma's and played with the kids on her block, but was constantly thinking about my new friends at my own home. Mom got off work at 3:00 p.m. and I was home by 4:00 p.m. Mom would cook dinner while I would go run, laugh, ride my bike, play with dolls, sit and have conversations, and hang out with MY FRIENDS. The experience was new to me, and I was loving every bit of it.

One Saturday, I woke up excitedly awaiting what was sure to be another great day. Per usual, I was not allowed out before noon. At noon, I headed out to greet my new friends. To my surprise, when I walked out the door, I was greeted by a "We Hate Ebony Parade." Yep, you read that right, an entire parade. Anitra had once again rallied the troops only this time there was an all-out assault on me. I was across the street sitting on the porch of my parents' two-bedroom home, that they'd recently added a dormer to, holding in the tears and wondering what I had done so bad that there was a parade about hating me. They marched up and down the street, created chants about hating me, taunted me saying that they would never play with me again, and even pointed and laughed at me. My heart ached. I'd given my all to these girls. I was sincere in wanting to be the best friend I could be. *Hadn't I shown them this through playing my heart out, always being available, and participating in all the conversations they wanted to have?*

Our parents would eventually intervene, and we would play together again, but things were never the same. I moved from that block just two years later and never talked to any of them again, although my parents continued their relationship with their parents for several years. That type of experience would raise its ugly head repeatedly later in my personal and professional life. Time and time again, I experienced similar situations where I committed to a group of girls and they would eventually turn on me. It happened enough that I started asking myself, *what is wrong with me?* When I'd let down my guard with a group of women in the area of friendship, it would most often end with a "we hate Ebony" parade of sorts. Those types of experiences caused She to take over more and more each time.

She learned to smile through painful situations. I remember smiling during my freshman year of college and pretending I didn't hear the snickers and whispers of lies being told on me. I learned to pretend I didn't care when I was included and pretended not to care about the lies, but it all hurt. When there was a co-ed group in high school that everyone applied to be a part of and all of my teammates were accepted except me (and got really cool jackets and was able to sit together at pep rallies), I pretended it didn't bother me. If memory serves me correctly, I think I may have been the only applicant that didn't get in. I remember ignoring the pain and self-doubt that set in later in life when line after line of sorority girls crossed and I was left to simply celebrate but with no letters of my own. I remember celebrating the others while wondering why I'd been looked over for promotions that I clearly deserved. It seemed as though with each passing year She became a larger part of my life.

Chapter Three

SISTER GIRL

The ultimate dichotomous existence was in the career world. Little did I know my experiences in early life were preparing me to stand in the spaces I'd be a part of for decades to come. As I ascended the corporate ladder, I was excited. I was making people proud. I was proud. I'd become an example for others to follow. I'd even gotten to the point where I could make demands. I'd become the voice for things that my people needed like pointing out that we should have more intern applicants from HBCUs or advocating for Black women in lower ranks that were being looked over.

I felt respected by my peers of all races, genders, ethnicities, socioeconomic status, etc. I'd often receive compliments from my managers. I'd built a solid reputation for being creative, confident, strategic, integrous, and was known for getting the job done. I'd even noticed that I'd become an unspoken fixer. If a department needed some TLC, needed to be turned around, or just needed some "heart" injected into it, I was your girl. One of the few awards I ever won was actually for leading from the heart. It was not lost on me while doing all of this that it was not just about me. It was about every Black person that set foot in the doors of whatever organization I was a part of, especially the Black women, and they often let me know it.

My ascension was fairly swift, but always marred with the negative interaction with the other Black girl. Yes, I had negative experiences with other men and women of all races, but I was always able to strategically navigate those interactions. The ones with the other Black women hurt. *These were supposed to be my sisters, right? We were supposed to live by the unspoken rules of protecting one another, right? There was supposed to be a code, right?* Time and time again it failed me. While I could read the white man for filth, in a professional manner of course; remind a superior of my boundaries and how they were not to be crossed, professionally of course; and utilize care and compassion as I held those subordinates to me accountable for not meeting the mark, in the most tender way of course; it was those same interactions with some Black women that I struggled with the most. Some of my sisters were on the same page as me and those interactions were what kept me going, but when I struggled it was bad. I struggled because I just cared too much. I wanted the sisterhood to exist so badly. I wanted to create bonds that could not be broken.

Let's be clear, not all of the relationships I'd had at work with Black women were bad. I had really great relationships that lasted a long time—mentors, mentees, and friends. At my first job, I met Sharon and Janet. While neither ever worked in the same department as me, they looked and saw a young sister and really poured into me as my mentors and big sisters. Sharon would introduce me to people, take me out on assignment with her to show me another side of the business, and even tell me the things I didn't want to hear but needed to hear. Sharon was the topic of the first article I wrote for my employer on mentorship. Janet made sure I had someone to eat with. She would come to church with me and allowed me the honor of working with her on her daughter's graduation party. Sharon and Janet were amazing mentors and I periodically hear from them even to this day. I literally had some of the best mentees a girl could ever have. They worked hard, were okay taking advice, and even during the rough times would have the real conversations. I appreciated several of them so much for being in my life. Even though I was technically their mentor, they taught me a ton as mentees. There was of course Kim and Christol, two of the best friends a girl could have. They'd moved on to other companies, but we kept the friendships going. These ladies were all great, but I'd experienced the other side of the relationships with Black women at work too. Many of them caused me to bury myself a little more and allow the representative out.

The first corporate role I had straight out of college lasted four years. In those four years, I received three promotions. The last promotion landed me right on the team of another Black woman. For the first time in my life, I was led by another Black woman. Surely, she would get me. I had dreams of her taking me under her wing and showing me the ropes. That dream was short lived and would ultimately end in a nightmare that caused me to type a resignation letter and walk out without a plan for the next steps of my journey.

I was hired to do business and technical writing. My first assignment was to write a training manual for a new process we would be following in our project management office. Easy peasy, or so I thought. I took my time, dissected the process, and went to work on the manual. I poured my heart into this manual. It was gorgeous. I'd even spent time researching the newest features of the word processing software so I could utilize graphics in the best possible way. I expected edits and changes to be necessary, but what I could not have expected was the delivery of those items.

During our weekly staff meeting when we reviewed the status of the projects we were working on, I was happy to announce to the team that I'd submitted the first draft of the manual for review and while waiting on the review I'd moved on to the next project at hand. After my status update, our manager, the other Black woman, took a printed document from her folder. At the time, I could not see what it was, I could just see that she had used so much red ink marking it up that whatever it was would need a lot of work to get it to where she wanted it to be. Just as I was wondering what it was, she flung it across the table at me and stated, in the most disrespectful tone, "I went through your draft and to be honest, if I have to do this much editing, I might as well do it myself." I heard her words, but at that moment, I couldn't respond. I was steaming, shaking, reeling from the fact that she'd just flung a packet of papers across the table at me. Remember that girl that grew up with her dad's side of the family that could string together words and fought if they needed to? That girl was on her way out. That girl was going to jump across that table and let this woman have it. But that other girl that grew up with her mom's side of the family that was proper and polite stopped her from doing that. I just sat there. I really can't even tell you what was discussed during the rest of the meeting. *Why would my sister do that to me? If it was that bad, she couldn't have just told me in private and helped me?* At that moment, I vowed to help every Black woman I came across in my career. I would never be the sister that forgot where she came from and treated Black women badly in the workplace.

When the meeting was over, I stood up and told her, "you need to stay behind for a moment!" The tension in the room could be cut with a knife as the rest of the staff exited the meeting. I proceeded to tell her, "if you ever throw anything at me again, I will jump across the table on you and we will be like two women fighting in the street." Not my finest career moment, but it happened. She was flabbergasted that I would speak to her in that manner and maintained that she did not throw anything at me. A few weeks later, things had spiraled, and I went to my desk, typed my resignation letter, and walked out. I remain on the "do not rehire" list for that organization to this day.

I've run into her several times since then. She always smiles and is polite. We exchange pleasantries and go our separate ways, but the pain from that day remains. The mentorship, the support, the relationship I'd hoped for with her didn't come from her. It came from a white woman, Peggy. Just before the promotion that would land me on her team, I'd met Peggy in my last department. Peggy was there for me, she taught me the unspoken rules of the department (she was about six months from retirement), she took me to the driving range because she said deals were made on the golf course and with my skill set, I'd find myself in executive offices one day that required I head to the golf course. She even gifted me the use of one of her rental condos at a golf and ski resort for my birthday weekend and awakened the appetite I now have for investing in real estate. She taught me many unspoken rules of engagement. I will forever be grateful to Peggy for that tutelage but longed for it to come from one of my own.

Later in my career, I'd moved through a few entry level

leadership roles at small companies and even struck out on my own for a while and had landed a pretty good paying consulting gig. I'd been hired to help the owner of a small real estate development firm determine the root of its culture problems. It took me about a week to determine the issue was the owner's mistress. He paraded her around the office as if no one knew. He pretended she was just his chief of staff; however, because of the way she treated everyone in the office, the fight she had with his wife in the parking lot, and the fact that she was often seen going into his private residence on the property and staying there overnight, and everything else that they, were sloppy, with it was obvious. I had a choice; I could be honest and help him understand what everyone was confiding in me or I could make something up and just get paid and move on. It was not in me to make things up, so I prepared my report and delivered it, knowing she would get to review it as well. The chief of staff reviewed the report and before I knew it, my assignment was ended. My contract was paid out, but here I was finding myself in the crosshairs of yet another Black woman.

Even though I'd experienced those things, career wise things were going well for me. I eventually landed in an organization where I'd spend quite a few years, as the growth potential was amazing. In this company, I ascended very quickly as well. During a stop at the mid-career level, another Black woman was moved to my team. "Ebony, you have a very genuine way of holding people accountable and making sure they live up to their potential, you coach them up or coach them out, so we believe you are just the leader that [this individual] needs." *Was this a compliment, sure, but why the hell hadn't her previous leaders been made to hold her accountable for her actions. Why weren't they held accountable for not holding her accountable?* That is okay, as a Black woman, she will understand that we have to stick together and for both of us and every other Black woman in the company that aspires to be where we are, she will turn it around or so I'd hoped. Unfortunately, it didn't happen, she continued her antics and I was faced with a choice, either hold her accountable to her actions or risk my own reputation. I decided I'd give it one last try. I called her into the office and said, "look, this is the last time we are going to have this conversation, you have either got to pull it together or there will be consequences." Another not so fine moment professionally. The other woman didn't appreciate the tone I took with her, and we quickly ended the conversation. Although she was angry and so was I, I thought that maybe that had been enough to save the situation.

It was not, and I would eventually have to demote her. I did what I had to do, but it was extremely hurtful. I remember crying for several nights after I'd demoted her because she was my sister. I needed her to succeed as much as I needed to succeed myself. We all needed her to succeed. I finally was able to reconcile things with myself after writing as usual. These are the words I wrote at that moment.

> *I don't usually cry about work-related stuff. Despite being a crybaby in the rest of my life, I try to stay very objective at work. I keep my personal life personal, and I try really hard to not get emotional about anything at work, but this one…this one hurt. I can't stop crying. I am so pissed off right now. I am pissed off at her. I am pissed off at them, and I think I am pissed off at myself for being in this damn situation in the first place.*

As a 40+ year old woman raising two kids on your own, making 6-figures, how the hell do you risk it all for Facebook!!! I mean I like to catch up on Facebook, too, but I'll be damn if I am going to stay on it all day to the detriment of my job. And I get having an illness that stops you from doing some things, but staying on that freakin' phone all the time makes it hard to believe that you are having a problem versus just being lazy. I told you…I told you as plainly as I could. When I said, "this is the last time we are going to have this conversation," I thought it was clear that if I had to talk to you about being on your phone, not tending to your team, or continuing to miss days that seem to be in a pattern of days coupled with weekends that your job was in jeopardy. I thought you would understand Black woman to Black woman that the last thing I wanted to have to do was to demote you. Damn you for putting me in this position.

And damn every leader that ever led you before me. I am so sick of everyone gathering in rooms to talk about what people are doing wrong but not taking any action to make it better. I am so tired of being the one known to take action. Why do we all have the same title and make the same money if you can't do the job. Hell, to be honest, most of you are probably making more than me with less experience and education but I have to be the one known for holding people accountable. Better yet, how the hell do these people keep getting promoted. I promise it boggles my mind that we are the #1 company in our industry with the number of unqualified people at the helm of some of these teams. So for years, this girl has been known as causing trouble by not doing what she was supposed to do, staying on her phone, and overall just not living up to her abilities. Yet, whomever happened to be in charge at the time just decided to shuffle her from leader to another leader to see if she gets better on her own. How is she gonna get better when everyone is scared to say anything to her and just lets her get away with it? How is she gonna get better when y'all all hang out at the bar with her and get drunk with her? How is she gonna get better when she witnesses a group of friends just constantly get promoted despite the fact that it could be other qualified candidates? How is it that I get to be the Black woman demoting another Black woman because no one else had the nerve to do it themselves? I'm just so damn irritated.

I am so frustrated with myself. I have cried and cried. I keep asking myself – how did you allow yourself to get in this position where you are the only one holding people accountable and you end up needing to demote another Black woman. How have you not made any noise about this and allowed this fiasco to continue to play out in front of your eyes. Yes, you need the money, yes you and Q have plans for the kids and the future that depend on this check, but is it worth it? Can you continue to hurt like this? It is one thing to be true to yourself and you are, but it is another for your genuine nature to be weaponized and that is how I feel. I am so angry. How do I continue to be what I believe is the best leader I can be and be surrounded by folks who won't live up to the expectations of what I think leadership is— leading, coaching, and making sure people are getting better.

I just don't know what to do with all of this emotion. Crying is all I can come up with right now. I am shedding tears of anger...anger with everyone involved. I am shedding tears of pain...pain to see another Black woman lose her job and pain that I had to be the one to do it. I am shedding tears of doubt...doubt that I can find a place that will ever fully see me for the whole me. I am shedding tears of confusion...do I stay here and continue to do the best I can do because I need the money despite knowing I am not being paid fairly based on my education and experience and quite frankly my performance? I just can't stop the tears from falling.

I can only pray that this anger, pain, frustration, and confusion will be clarified through these tears I am continuing to cry. Dear God, please help me...what do I do next?

I am reminded of several white men that have thanked me for my guidance, for being stern with them, for holding them accountable for their actions. One in particular told me that he went home angry and told his wife about the conversation I'd had with him to which his wife responded, "was she telling the truth, though? Are those things that you need to work on?" He thanked me for no longer allowing the foolishness to continue. I remember running into one of my former trainers who said, "do you remember day one when you set me straight, and let me know you were not going to deal with any of my antics? I really appreciate that; you are definitely missed by our teams." If they realized I wanted to help and not harm them, why had my sister not seen it? Why had she not just stopped the foolishness, she was so talented.

Unfortunately, she would later go on to resign from the organization. I ran into her a few times, once at a funeral. We embraced and cried together at the loss of our co-worker that kept us laughing. I ran into her walking her dogs in the morning and exchanged pleasantries. I truly wished things had turned out differently. The pain of hurting another Black woman through demotion remains with me.

I was once given a gift that I am sure many Black women professionals dream of— a promotion to lead a team made up of mostly Black women. Excited doesn't begin to explain my feeling going into this new role. I had dreams of us being a powerhouse team. I was accepted with open arms. I was showered with compliments, and praise and comments such as, "we are so happy to have you." I was proud of my self-proclaimed dream team, and we went to work, looking to change the world, revive the reputation of the area, and make an impression on the organization that would be remembered for years to come. I tried really hard to coach, be honest, and make sure these women were given all they deserved. I created positions for some who'd been looked over for far too long, gave out raises to those that were woefully under paid, and let my hair down just a bit because we shared the commonality of Black womanhood. But just as before, it ended in a "we hate Ebony" parade. I had no idea that the tide was going to shift, but it did. I'd let my guard down, given all I had to these relationships I tried to mentor, develop, and learn myself only to be made out to be the villain in the end. I was proud of the work, proud to level salaries for these women, proud to be able to give out well deserved promotions for which they'd been passed over (unfairly) for in the past. But I hadn't learned that none of this would earn me a space to tell the truth or even to act as a protector.

The unraveling started with a resignation. One Friday evening, I was at my weekly volunteer event when I received a call from Human Resources telling me that someone would be essentially placed on administrative leave. Unbeknownst to me, there was a full-on investigation happening with one of my direct reports of which I had no awareness. The following Monday I was brought up to speed on the happenings and I went into full on protection mode. I was losing the fight of what was going to turn into a termination, and I could see that, so I went to plan B, fighting for severance including medical benefits and out placement services. When I finally won that fight, left the office I'd been in for hours and headed to my office, I was greeted with "have you seen this." The very person I was fighting for had resigned, posted her resignation on social media, and from the grapevine blamed me for causing the investigation to kick off when I in fact was not made aware until it was damn near complete. I later found out that the investigation was sparked by one of her colleagues but that was nothing I could reveal. I found out that this group of women often had conversations about me, referring to me in code and having full out gossiping sessions about me. While I was working hard on their behalf, they were prepping signs of their parade.

One of these ladies was promised a higher title with a reorganization (I didn't make the promise). When the person who made the promise didn't make good on it, I was once again blamed, although I had nothing to do with it. I didn't promote another because I knew that the role that she was applying for would be extremely high stress (something she was not prepared for) and would require she work with individuals that did not speak highly of her (a position that only lasted a year and would have resulted in her eventual demotion or termination), but I was again the culprit accused of having it out for her versus the person attempting to protect her career reputation. She eventually left the company a year or two later and rumor had it, she left because of me. There was yet another promotion gone awry when two of them would be up for the same role.

In the end, the "we hate Ebony parade" was there yet again, as I'd have to work with all of these ladies in the future but could no longer trust most of them and knew that I was the topic of many of their conversations. While my professional reputation was intact, because they'd marred theirs long before I crossed their paths and I'd in fact been warned not to put in so much work with them as individuals, it still hurt tremendously and caused me to remember why I'd always kept a wall up that I didn't allow people to climb in professional settings.

The executive ranks would be different though, *right?* There were very few of us there and if we were there, we were sure to have experienced the same things, *right?* We would definitely have an unwritten code, one that we would hold tight to because it would lend itself to what we spent our careers fighting for, representation, *right?* I'd met many along the way that were amazing. Some of these women I still keep in touch with even though we no longer work in the same fields, no longer have the same career trajectories, and no longer are on the same path. We periodically share a glass of wine and exchange stories about how we wish things in our respective careers could be different with our sisters.

There have also been some more instances where I'd had to hold my sisters accountable or didn't support the promotion someone thought I should have supported and they bad-mouthed me for it, but that was part of the job. They weren't the only ones. People of all genders, ethnicities, sexual identities, etc. had been frustrated with me when I called them out for their foolishness, challenged the way they'd always done things, or taken some form of disciplinary action. I'd learned that was the nature of the beast if I remained in the executive ranks and I performed the duties of the job well. I was always a woman of character, my credibility was intact, and my integrity impeccable. I knew I wasn't perfect, but I tried hard to do and be my best. But none of that could prepare me for what I would experience among the executive ranks.

Among the executive ranks, I would experience what I believed to be the ultimate betrayal from one of my sisters. To stay true to who I am and to not have a negative impact on the career of another sister, I will keep the details vague, but I will express every detail of the pain and suffering the incident caused me. I remember putting my trust in three women. We'd met a few times, and all decided that we needed to come together, create a proposal, and present it to our superiors for approval. Before that could happen one of the women chose to leave the company, we were all employed by and we found ourselves in the midst of a global pandemic. In the midst of the global pandemic, like many things, this pet project took a back seat.

After months of being inside our homes and isolated from

most, I'd successfully defended my dissertation virtually. I needed a change of scenery and so did my family, but where could we go with this deadly virus circling the globe? We decided to pack up the car and drive to the Great Smoky Mountains. We'd shared many fun times there in the past and it would be a perfect getaway. We loaded up the car and headed out. We spent a week in a beautiful cabin just outside of Gatlinburg, TN. We cooked together, we fished together, we explored the mountains together, just the five of us. I remember heading home feeling refreshed and renewed. I didn't know what was waiting for me upon my return. Just as I was returning, I received a phone call the Sunday before I returned to work from my vacation. The idea that the three of us had previously said we'd work on together and present together was coming to fruition. The issue was that we'd not met about it in months, and we hadn't put the proposal together. I thought we were all head down working on surviving a pandemic, but somehow one of the ladies had managed to discuss the project with the higher ups without the rest of us. Maybe she presented a proposal, maybe she just had a conversation, maybe it was brought to her, and she just took the ball and ran with it. No matter how it fell in her lap, what I do know is that she had not acknowledged that we'd all discussed this endeavor, hadn't insisted that we be included in the discussions, and hadn't at least talked to us before everything was all planned out if the higher ups had come to her with the idea and chosen her to lead the charge. We should have all been a part of building this together. The reality is that I don't know if any of us was really qualified to lead the charge the way it needed to be led, and I was of the opinion that someone from the outside with no established alliances would be best to make sure we had the best outcomes, but if it was going to be someone from inside, we all should have been considered equally and at least given a chance.

The call came from her to inform me of the project and how it would impact my life only AFTER it was all in motion. As she explained the details of what was to come, I held it together as best I could. I was polite, professional, and courteous but I was devastated. While the idea was not mine alone, we'd all agreed to work on it together. While I believed in the what, I, in no way shape or form believed in the *how* it was happening. Now, somehow, she'd taken it and was at the helm. This was her baby and I and the other lady involved would receive consolation prizes in this competition that I did not know was a competition. In retrospect, I should have stood my ground when given the chance and said, "no, this is wrong, and I won't be a part of it," but I did not, and I paid the price daily with my emotional health.

I wish I could say that I have reconciled my feelings in this situation, but I have not. As I have watched this idea unfold and catapult her into spaces, place her on stages, and provide opportunities for her that I believe should have been all of ours or at the very least should have been won by running a race we all knew we were running; I remain angry about it. Let's be clear, I have expressed how I feel to those that needed to know. I have had many conversations about the feelings I harbor in this situation. I have not kept them to myself. We have both moved on to do other things in our careers and both are doing quite well for ourselves, but that betrayal stays with me. We are courteous, cordial, and professional in each other's presence, and have even enjoyed some moments of laughter and light heartedness since the situation unfolded, but I am doubtful there will ever be a relationship of substance between us because the voice in the back of my mind reminds me of the situation and how it unfolded with each of our interactions. It hurt to think that I'd once again trusted only to be hurt by a sister.

The experiences I had with other black women were not all negative. In fact, many were positive, but from the very first "we hate Ebony parade" the sting of my negative experiences with other Black women hurt much worse than any other. I'm not sure why, but I knew it was something that I had to work through, and I needed to work at it in therapy. Those were not the only experiences that led to the burial of some of the brightest spots of Ebony, there were others that not only contributed but had just as large of an impact on me and contributed to the mental and emotional issues I was experiencing. But believing that I should be my sister's keeper and her mine, I in some ways felt like the comedian Mo'Nique— betrayed, labeled, and dismissed so that others could hide their own imperfections or wrongs. It hurt!

Chapter Four

WE'RE AT WAR

If you are reading this book, there is a good chance that you remember exactly where you were on September 11, 2001, during the devastating terror attacks on the World Trade Center. I remember where I was. I was standing in the small convenience store in the lower level of my office building, surrounded by cookies, coffee, breakfast sandwiches, and other small snack type items. There was a small black and white portable television in the corner that always had the news or a talk show playing, depending on the time of day you entered the shop. Most mornings the television provided background noise, but on that day, it was the main source of information for everyone within listening and viewing distance. We all stood frozen and confused. Like many corporations, the organization I worked for at the time, dismissed us all and I went straight home to my mom's. My safe space to this day.

You may not remember the date of August 14, 2003, but if you lived anywhere on the east coast or in the Midwest you will remember the Great Black Out and where you were when all the lights went out. I was with a friend scoping out properties for her dream of opening a spa. We entered the property knowing that there was no electrical service currently in the building, but it was daytime, and we were with the realtor. As we left the property and the realtor was locking up, we noticed there had been a pretty bad car accident about a block away that had taken out a utility pole, so as we proceeded to drive through the neighborhood, we assumed that was the cause for the traffic lights in the immediate area being out. We continued to our final destination to a shoe store about three miles away. We were so engulfed in talking about our dreams and the businesses that we would own, it did not hit us until we arrived at the shoe store that there had been no traffic lights the entire way; that was strange. We then entered the shoe store, and there were no lights. *Wait a minute, what was going on?*

The owner of the shoe store was listening to a battery-operated radio and informed us that power was out on the entire east coast and in the Midwest. Since we couldn't use our cell phones, she took me to my car and we both hurried to our safe spaces. For me, it was once again my parents' house. While we'd never discussed it, my husband and brothers all instinctively knew my parents' home would be the meeting place and within a matter of about an hour the entire family had gathered in that safe space. Like with many people, I have a safe space, my mother's home. It brings me comfort; I know there will always be a meal waiting or one cooked when I arrive. Whether we are laughing, crying, praying, cooking, or arguing, I know that is a place where family will be and the love will overflow.

So, on March 12, 2020, I did what I often did on weeknights, I ran by my mom's to pick up the kids (she got them from school for me daily). I ate and headed home. It was a little strange because our organization had decided we'd work from home for two weeks to "test" our systems and ensure they could handle any emergency situation that required us to be home longer. The work still had to get done. Over the weekend the details around the impending impact the spreading global pandemic was having was intensifying. Schools canceled classes, businesses closed, and shelter in place orders were going into effect in other parts of the country. March 16, 2020, I'd taken the day off because it was my wedding anniversary and I always spend that day with my husband, but by that morning it was clear things were going to be different for a while. At that time, I held the title of VP of Learning and Development, we had several training classes starting and they would all need to go from in person to online. We would have to determine how to get new hires equipment or let them utilize their own, make sure that all of our trainers had a space to train from inside of their homes, we had to make sure we could account for everyone, and strategize. Strategy is a strength of mine, so I leapt into action. That day, my 18th wedding anniversary, I didn't spend time with my husband. I spent it telling him continuously until he stopped asking, "give me 30 minutes and I promise I'll be done here." That day I also didn't go to mom's; I didn't go to my safe space.

One week later, the first shelter in place order for our state went into place. It was scary. I had no room to be scared, though, I needed to be strong. I needed to make sure that my family was okay. I needed to make sure that my team was okay. I needed to make sure that everyone around was okay. I could check on me later. I started to strategize and plan like never before. At home, I planned several activities to keep the kids busy when they weren't in online class - cooking competitions, fake interviews for jobs in the house, game and movie nights, home improvement projects that we could work on as a family, outdoor tent parties, anything I could think of to keep an eleven-year-old and fourteen-year-old occupied for a few weeks because surely this would be over soon.

My husband is a contractor and work came to an abrupt halt for him. He is not the kind to sit still so I knew this would be difficult for him. I also knew that music is often healing for him, so I bought the largest speaker system I could find for our outdoor patio and deck area and had it delivered to the house for him. My neighbors might not have liked it, but my husband needed it so they had to deal with it. I'd already anticipated the need for more food when I'd learned we'd be home for a few weeks so our fridge, pantry, two freezers, and toiletry closet were well stocked. I'd taken care of that mid-week. If you wanted to eat it, cook it, needed to clean with it, or needed it for hygiene purposes, I had bought it and a lot of it. I wanted my family to be safe and have everything to make them feel comfortable. I wanted our home to be a safe space and so I did all I could to create that space.

At work, I went into hyper strategy or hyper overdrive mode if that is a thing. I needed a strategy for everything. I was responsible for our training team. The team that these new hires would see online, my team, would give them the first glimpse into the world of our employer. My team would keep the trains on the tracks. We would have to get new hires up and running and also cross-train current employees to make sure that we could keep the company running. My team might have been the smallest team of my division, but I was determined we would have a mighty impact during this time. In hindsight, I can see how my actions may have seemed as though I was over doing it, but I really just cared so much.

I scheduled a fifteen-minute virtual morning huddle for the start of every day, cameras on! I wanted to investigate the faces of each individual and make sure they were okay, I needed them to feel safe. I popped into virtual training classes and required my immediate direct reports to do the same to see how it was going, making sure cameras were on. I needed the trainees to be safe. I called my staff every day just to check in on them and even scheduled fun virtual events. I needed to look at them and make sure they were safe. For two months, I poured everything I had into trying to make sure everyone I knew felt safe. Making sure they were safe made me feel safe.

May 25, 2020 – 7 minutes and 46 seconds of video emerged. 7 minutes and 46 seconds pulled me out of the false sense of safety that I was trying to create. 7 minutes and 46 seconds that depicted a phenomenon that was not new to me as a Black woman but seemed to be new to many I encountered in the workspace. In the days and weeks that followed, there were multiple travesties unfolding. There was the senseless murder of yet another Black man that was revealed in 7 minutes and 46 seconds of video footage showing the senseless death of George Floyd – that was the obvious tragedy. But then there was the tragedy of the seemingly unending continuous "public lynching," as my good friend, Paula, describes it, of Black men at the hands of white cops. Lynchings that we as Black people had to watch consistently, mask the severe grief we felt with each of these stories and somehow pull ourselves together to go to work the next day. This time the difference was that I was asked to speak about it. It was being recognized across the country because we were all in our homes away from our day-to-day routines, so it could not be ignored. The media coverage was nonstop. Something had to be done. I was asked to share my feelings on the topic in a large corporate gathering, and I did. I was honest, moved to tears as I expressed that I didn't buy the house I wanted to buy because my little Black boys would one day be driving, and buying that house I wanted would require them to drive through all white neighborhoods and that scared me because a cop might kill them. I shared the deep-rooted fear that I have every time my husband is thirty minutes late coming home. Not a fear that he was in an accident or doing something wrong, but the fear that some cop would have him on the side of the road with a knee in his neck. I was as open, honest, and raw as I could be while the tears streamed down my face. I then remembered telling my boss that I didn't want to come to work the next few days because I was emotionally spent. I needed to sit with my emotions and process all that had happened. She was supportive and told me to take all the time I needed.

However, as I reflect on that situation, the nerve of anyone to expect all of us as Black people to instantly be willing to share the depths of our feelings on the racists disregard for human life that we feared and carried with us daily was unfathomable. The thought that the spaces being created for us to share -- were safe spaces -- was, in a nutshell, bullshit! Her intentions were the very best, but the impact of those intentions I now know were harmful to me and many others. Had I been able to process it all in that moment, I would have had the conversation with her and I am sure she would have understood, but I wasn't able to process it so I just pushed through like I always did. As one of my co-workers always said, I did not secure my oxygen mask first!

I didn't realize what was happening in those moments, but

now I realize my emotional safe space had been stripped away, and I'd been a willing participant to the stripping. No matter how pure the intention to empathize and create the space, it was being stripped away. No human being can experience severe, prolonged, masked grief and expect that a meeting, book club, or creation of a DEI office would heal the wound instantly. For the next few days, I sat on my deck for most of the day trying my hardest to process the senseless murder, the feelings it evoked inside of me, how I'd return to work after the raw show of emotion I'd just displayed, and how I could make a difference, so things didn't just go back to the status quo. Eventually, I had to pull it together, tuck away whatever emotions I had, try not to be triggered, and be the leader I'd been trained to be.

I did just that, tucked away my emotions, led my teams, and when triggered, I only shared it with those closest to me in an effort for some relief. As the days, weeks, and months continued, we continued to have shelter in place orders. The death toll of the COVID-19 pandemic continued to rise with a disproportionately high percentage of deaths being in the Black community. My husband was still unable to work. My children would need to do the entire next year of school virtually. I would not be able to see many of my friends for well over a year as our family opted to only interact with one another because of my mom's compromised immune system and our desire to protect her at all costs. My nephew was unable to have a senior prom or graduation. I continued to attend all corporate events, from the day-to-day meetings to the annual award ceremony, relegated to the black box assigned to me by Zoom, Teams, Google Meet, or whatever the software of choice would be at that time.

One day as I did what I do, put on a happy face and interact with my kids in their makeshift classroom that was once my dining room, my daughter said to me, "Mommy, I never thought I'd live through a war in my lifetime." I was baffled, *what war was she talking about?* I asked, "babe, what war are you talking about?" She said, "COVID-19 – I can't see my friends, I can't go anywhere, we don't have any extracurricular activities, I can't have fast food, I can't go to the grocery store, I have to take Grandma's tonic every day and Daddy makes us stand over citrus steams in the kitchen every morning. Mommy, Daddy can't work, you stay in your office all day working, we even have to wash all the groceries before they come in the house, and people are dying!" At that moment, I realized she was right. We were at war. COVID-19 was a war that we didn't see coming but now we were fighting with everything we had. The mental and emotional toll of the pandemic would far out live and outweigh the extremely crippling devastation of the death toll. It would prove to be difficult for all people, but for Black people it would have effects that words cannot describe, and for years to come. For me, the impact was tremendous.

The COVID-19 war became the second war that I was fighting. I was fighting two wars, the war that I'd fought day in and day out for years…the war of being a Black woman in corporate America that required all my strength, all my armor and every tool I'd amassed through obtaining three degrees, working in multiple corporate arenas, raising a family, being an entrepreneur, and most importantly being a Christian woman. Now I needed to find more to fight yet a second war and be even stronger for my family. I dug deep and found it, but when it was over, I was empty, I had nothing more to give to anyone. I had nothing to give to my children, my husband, my family, my teams, myself, my God. And the wheels started to fall off.

Chapter Five

TRYING TO FIND A NEW NORMAL

Turned out that I worked from home full time for about a year and a half. My children finished their 7th and 10th grade years completely online (I could write an entire book about that experience alone, and I am sure someone has). My husband could not work for almost a year. Everything stopped but continued at hyper speed all at the same time, yet another dichotomous experience. The outside world was on pause, but in our capitalistic society, the money had to continue to be made, and the children had to continue to be herded through our educational system like cattle. We now lived in a society where technological advancements made sure that the wheels kept turning whether it was in a physical high touch environment or virtually. The work would be done. For a while I didn't even think about it, it was just what needed to be done.

During this time, there were some major issues coming to light for me. First, as a self-described extroverted-introvert, I needed my quiet time, time away from everything to just sit with myself to reflect, to pray, to meditate, and just be with Ebony. Second, the use of technology created the ability to work from home, but it also created a powerful intrusion into my personal space that I'd worked really hard to keep separate from my professional life. Last, but possibly contributing most to what I would experience in 2023, was yet another dichotomous experience. As the world tried to return to normal, I needed to be okay with returning to the workplace and working amongst people, supporting those people at the same time that I had to be okay with working from home and supporting those that were not yet ready to return to the workplace. I was yet again unseen as no one asked, considered, or even wondered what I needed, but I had to be the most visible person for all my team members and I was so used to that being the case, I saw nothing wrong with it while it was happening.

As an introvert, I am often misunderstood. Since I have created an alter ego that can push into an outgoing space to deliver speeches, to interact in executive crowds, or to be on the arm of the social butterfly that I am married to and be social with the best of them. Many people believe that deep down I am an extrovert that can get into a funky mood and not want to be bothered with people. The reality is that I am an introvert that is often completely drained by being outside of my comfort zone to satisfy the needs of the outside world, and I just needed time alone to recharge that battery.

I spoke to another mom at an extracurricular event and our conversation brought her to tears as I told her how much I just really loved her son's spirit. He is polite, he is caring, he is such a gentle spirit in a brutal world. She was not brought to tears because of the compliment. She was brought to tears because in her words, "I hope he is going to be okay, he is such a loner." I responded by explaining that I was a loner as well, I was an introvert as well, and I was just fine. I know a lot of people and interact with a lot of people, but I could definitely be a loaner. She told me that she could see that in me, but that she was just worried that her child would miss out on opportunities because of his introversion. I tried to encourage her by telling her that other introverts would see him and look out for him. I was telling her what I'd hoped for my entire career. I longed for people to just understand that I'd do the job and it would be spectacular, but I needed my me time and I did not want to be bombarded with the "whatcha got up after work" invites that often led to places I didn't want to be.

During the pandemic, that recharge time did not exist. I went from my bed to my shower, from my shower to my kitchen to prepare breakfast, from my kitchen to my home office to work, from my home office to my kitchen to prepare lunch and/or dinner, from my kitchen back to my office, from my office to my dining room table to help with homework or to some other part of the home to try to create family time, from my home to my mom's to check on her with kids in tow, from moms back to my home to prepare for the next day. I did that five days a week for over a year. On the weekend there were slight changes, but I was never alone physically or virtually.

For months, on the weekend one change was the half-day grocery run that required a full court press from the entire family. My husband and I would get up at the crack of dawn to go to the warehouse store and fill up for a couple of weeks, ensuring we were socially distanced and of course wore our masks and gloves.

We alerted the kids as we left. They knew that was their queue to clean and organize the fridge and pantry for the incoming groceries. They also knew that meant to make cleaning water for all the groceries that would need to be thoroughly sanitized before being placed in our home. In the winter months this was brutal but as a family we made it through. The rest of Saturday and some of Sunday were often used to catch up on work that I hadn't managed to finish during the grueling twelve-hour days I was already putting in. My then boss would schedule meetings before my workday usually started, after it usually ended, or get this part, on the weekend (or at least projects that were due that required I work on the weekend). Church was online and I rarely even dressed or got out of bed to hear the sermon. I'd turn on the phone and barely listen as I dreaded the service ending because that meant I needed to hop out of bed and get moving. For me as an introvert, there was no time to just be. No time to just sit and reflect. No time to recharge. To be honest, in retrospect, I am not sure how any person – introvert or extrovert – was supposed to continue to run at this clip and not spiral out of control. In my mind it was what had to happen and so I did it.

Technology made it so that the lines between work and home were not just blurred, they did not exist. Before 2020 when I got in my car and left the office at least there was some separation, even though the day's events, microaggressions I'd experienced, or some crazy story of a person who'd committed some egregious act but was saved because "they needed help" often followed me home to process, at least I was in my safe space to try to deal with it. You see, I am the girl that still carries two phones (one personal and one for work). When I got ready to put down the email, not see the text messages, and try to just focus on my personal life,

I would put the work phone in a different room or simply turn it off. It often caused me problems the next day because I didn't see the email that came through at 10 p.m., didn't respond to the funny group chat that everyone was trying to make a comment on at some ungodly hour, or was late to the "happy birthday" or "happy work anniversary" text, but I was okay with whatever the consequence was because I needed *separation of church and state.* Being home full time, that separation could no longer take place.

I would often be in another part of the house and hear the Microsoft Teams call sound coming from my computer and dart in to answer the call before I realized what I was doing. Work became such an intrusive part of my life. I can remember one day getting off work, taking off my bra, hearing the Teams call, and literally darting back into the office to answer the call. It was not until I saw myself on camera that I realized what I'd done and scrambled to cut the video feed. I was becoming more and more tired, more and more overwhelmed and therefore slipping into some pretty bad habits. I'd listen to morning status calls while in the shower or still in bed when I didn't need to be on camera. I was scheduling meetings around naps because I just couldn't stay awake. Things that came easy for me in the past were simply not easy anymore.

Our well-intentioned leadership team insisted on virtual team outings and got super creative with it. There were virtual cooking classes or virtual painting classes that would require me to be in my kitchen or another part of my home for work to spill over into. These events also invited my colleagues into other parts of my home, via the camera feed, something that I'd not been comfortable with, simply as a private person. I just want my home to be my safe space and for work not to spill over into it. In turn I was doing the same thing to my teams. I was forcing interaction down their throats. I was doing it because I cared, and my leaders were as well. What I didn't realize in the moment was that I was causing undue stress on top of the unexpected war we were already fighting. What I didn't learn, until later, was the stress that I caused myself and the impact it would eventually have on my mental health. I was not creating safe spaces. In fact, I was doing the opposite.

About eighteen months later, the inevitable happened. We returned to work in the office, the kids returned to school with extra-curriculars, and my husband returned to work. There were a few differences, the COVID-19 protocols required that we daily attested to not being positive for COVID-19 or being exposed to COVID-19. As usual, I did this for everyone in the house instead of expecting them to handle it for themselves. I also only returned to the office a couple days a week. It wasn't mandatory, but as an executive member of the team surely it wouldn't look good if I didn't show my face in the office. Not to mention, at that point I really wanted to see someone other than my family. But it was awkward, I am a hugger, but I couldn't hug people, I couldn't see their expressions, not everyone wanted to come back in the office, and what was I saying about supporting their beliefs or needs by being in the office myself? It was probably the most polarizing time I ever remember in a corporate space.

There was no time for me to process my own feelings, I simply had to perform. I had to do what was required of me in my role and She was good at it. While at home, my entire team had been moved to another company in our parent organization and I needed to fight for the understanding of what we did and how we did it. I needed to fight for the respect our team deserved, while simultaneously creating a strategy that would allow us to take advantage of the new environment we found ourselves in. I needed to keep going and be the consummate professional. Despite the continued issues that I faced as a Black woman in America, there was no time for the reconciliation of that existence. Despite being a believer often thrust into offensive conversations or situations, there was no time for the reconciliation of that existence. Despite the fact that I'd spent much of the pandemic in counseling with my husband, so we didn't allow this hurdle to destroy a decades long bond that we'd built, I didn't have time for individual therapy, there was no time to reconcile my individual needs. Despite the DEI departments created and promises made, when we returned to work the focus shifted from that work. I didn't have time for the reconciliation of that experience. I just had to keep going.

Chapter Six

HURDLES OR PROBLEMS

I didn't know it at the time, but while I kept going outwardly, I was slowly falling apart inwardly. I was falling apart physically, mentally, emotionally, and spiritually. If you are a Christian, you probably know the story of Doubting Thomas. Thomas was one of Jesus' twelve disciples. After the crucifixion and resurrection, when Jesus first went to visit the disciples, Thomas missed the entire celebration. When the other disciples told him that Jesus had returned, Thomas told them that he would believe it when he saw it with his own eyes, hence the nickname Doubting Thomas. But as Michael Todd so eloquently discusses in his sermon entitled *Snitches Get Stitches*, Thomas was hurt that he didn't get to see Jesus with the other disciples originally. As the story unfolds, Jesus returns to Thomas and allows him to see that it was really him that had returned from the dead. Mike

Todd asserts that Thomas was able to get his healing because Thomas was able to fall apart and show how he really felt. According to Pastor Todd, Doubting Thomas should really be known as Damaged Thomas because perhaps he was hurt and acted just as many of us would have had we been in the same situation, or as many of us do as we are hurt throughout our lives. I don't know if Thomas was hurt, or just not there. I don't know if Thomas was damaged or just doubting, but I realized I'd become Damaged Ebony.

I was falling apart physically. People that have known me for a while were witnessing a tremendous change in my health, both physically and mentally. I was tipping the scales at almost 200 pounds, 198 pounds to be exact. I remember thinking to myself, *as long as you don't get to 200 you can still turn it around,* all of this from the girl who'd fought to gain weight her entire life. What in the whole hell was I thinking, those two pounds didn't mean anything. I'd forgotten to care about my health. I was eating like crap at times and would find myself literally shoveling food in my mouth for comfort. I'd made jokes about how you could tell how bad my day was by the number of junk food wrappers you saw in my trash can or on my desk by the end of the day. I remember a time when sweets weren't even my thing, I just didn't enjoy them and now I was drinking my sweets through tons of juices, eating candy bars by the dozen, smashing family size bags of potato chips, and overeating like crazy.

I'd been diagnosed with type two diabetes with an HbA1c of 10.7%! That number is far too high and extremely bad. My blood was like Kool-Aid because it was so full of sugar. The HbA1c number reports the average blood sugar levels in a person over a 90-day period. Normal HbA1c readings, or what you will hear many diabetics and practitioners refer to as A1c is under 5.7% and you are diagnosed with diabetes at 6.5% or higher. My reading was at 10.7%. My doctor asked me things like "does your urine smell sweet?" In the moment, I was thinking *what the hell do you mean, does my urine smell sweet?* I didn't answer her question, but the reality was that part of the reason I was there was because my urine had a different smell and even my sweat had a different smell. In retrospect, I guess it could be described as sweet, I just didn't equate urine and sweat to anything sweet.

I cried in the office when I found out, learned to give myself insulin shots, and changed my diet momentarily, but I was so deep in at this point, I slipped right back into the junk. I'd always had textbook blood pressure readings, but not anymore. My blood pressure was elevated and I was now taking Lisinopril and Hydrochlorothiazide. The highest I can remember my blood pressure being was 147/92. While that is not alarming to most, it is super high for me. The textbooks will tell you that your blood pressure should be under 120/80 and up until this point in life my blood pressure remained great, but now things were just out of control. I couldn't sleep at night and was prescribed hydroxyzine to try to help me sleep. We'd also talked about the possibility of me utilizing melatonin or even cannabis. I was forty-eight years old and taking more daily medication than my mother who had survived cancer and two bone marrow transplants!

Mentally and emotionally, I was a wreck. I thought I was okay, but in reality, I was not okay. I smiled at work because I thought I had to. I smiled at events because I had to. I smiled at home because I thought I had to, but I was sad. A sad that I couldn't really explain. A sad that I now know as depression, that

I tried to keep buried, but that reared its ugly head at some of the most damaging times and with the people that I loved the most. I realized how I was showing up when my kids chuckled one day about how the house would shake when I would slam doors and about small things like dishes in the sink or the shoes they left out of place. I realized that my temper would flare up and go from zero to a thousand instantly. It wasn't the dishes in the sink, the clothes left too long in the washer, or anything that could be seen with the visual eye. It was the emptiness and sadness that I felt inside. The anger that I didn't believe that anyone saw me, really saw me. I remember being so sad that for days I'd cry myself to sleep, get up and cry through my shower, and then pull it together for the world to see a well put together executive because that is what She did.

I'd often cry through church services. People were used to me crying at church, so it was no big deal. They'd often say things like, "*we know how she is, she is going to cry anyway,*" or "*you know that if one of her kids testifies, she's going to cry.*" While those statements were true, they weren't the reason for the crying in those times. In those times, I didn't have anywhere else to place the emotion except in the bottled-up tears that had the opportunity to explode in church weekly. My husband knew what was happening and that this cry was different, and he just tried to console me as he always did. I was sure that Mom could tell what was happening from the look on her face, even from the pulpit. Moms have those intuitions and just know their babies, even when they are almost fifty-year-old babies. My mom often knew what was going on with me before I told her. As I mother, I know it is just mother's intuition. No matter how hard we try to hide things from our mothers about our emotions they pick up on the smallest of change in movement, a word you used, or a movement that just seemed different. They always knew, and as my mother studied my face and movements in these church crying spells, I knew—she knew—I was not okay.

I am sure one of my brothers could tell as well. We are not twins but we are twin souls. We were each other's only play mate for years, whenever either of us was in trouble the first person we called were each other. We always caught each other before a fall – he lived in my living room for six months and it was only fair since I crashed in his dorm room for an entire semester (imagine how difficult that had to be to have your older sister in your dorm room on a college campus). We knew each other's every move and he knew that this cry was not the same. It was not a cry that I could talk through or smile through or pull myself out of quickly. It was different and I am sure he knew it by the way he looked at me and asked if I was okay. Everyone else thought it was just the same old crybaby Ebony, but this was different. This sadness was taking over. Taking over in a way that didn't even allow me to worship the way I enjoyed.

My relationships were suffering. I thank God for a partner in life, a husband; a best friend who understands that there will be rough times and didn't just run out on me at the first sign of distress. When I tell y'all I gave this man the business…I mean I gave him the business. Not only did I expect him to care for me and be the loving caring person I married, but I expected him to comfort me in my sadness, understand my unreasonable tongue lashings when I was upset, cuddle with me when I needed and still date me, but be the sounding board for all the ridiculous thoughts and opinions I had during this time. I didn't have many friends and couldn't cultivate the friendships that I did have because I was busy doing all the things that I thought needed to be done. I couldn't build new friendships because I was busy doing all the things I thought needed to be done. I wasn't being the friend that I so desperately needed, so I couldn't expect anyone to reciprocate, but I am thankful for those that saw me and stayed around until I made it through.

Chapter Seven

THE TURNING POINT – KNOWING IS HALF THE BATTLE – THAT'S SOME BULLSHIT

It was April when the wheels really started to come off. My cousin closest to me in age, on my mom's side of the family, lost a long health battle and passed away. I was trying to figure out how to go to his funeral in North Carolina when I was told there would be a service in Dayton as well. Dayton is closer so I decided to go to Dayton whenever that took place. But because She needed the family to know she cared and supported them in the time of need, She streamed the NC service on the iPad at the bowling alley while my son was in league…who does that? She does because she has to make sure she shows up for everybody, right?

That same day while coming home from getting my eyebrows arched (something Ebony would love to do more often but She didn't have the time for that), I called to check in on my husband who was taking his turn sitting with his very ill ninety-four-year-old grandmother. "Hey babe, just checking in on you, seeing how the day is going." To which he responded, "Grandma passed." My heart broke for him, for his mom, for the entire family. The matriarch was gone. *Why hadn't I just gone with him that morning so he wouldn't have been there by himself!* I sped to his side. *I should have been there to begin with,* She told herself. *Why hadn't he called me?*

We watched while the body was removed from the home, we got food, we ate, we sat as a family. Late that night, on the way home I popped open Facebook just to browse, only to learn that another cousin of mine had been hit by a train while walking from the store in a freak accident. Damn! While I wasn't close to him, I often had great conversations with his mom and brother and my heart ached for them. I would consequently attend two more funerals and on back-to-back Saturdays because after he was hit his mom had a massive stroke and died the week after. *Jesus, what is going on?* Ebony thought as She just kept going.

The summer months that followed would be prom send off, high school graduation, open house, college orientation, getting her ready and dropping one of my heartbeats off at college on the other side of the country, making a way to get him to caddy training, helping with summer school, helping with the application to bowl out of state, making arrangements to bowl out of state, getting him organized for upcoming year, family reunion planning and hosting, ensuring a great internship experience for my interns, getting more involved with my community services, and so much more. All while the market took a hit and work slowed to a grinding halt and caused us not to receive cash bonuses for the first time in years (the year I actually planned to use it to pay college tuition), and we had to go through yet another work force reduction while adjusting to retirements of key figures at work and wondering what the next eighteen months would look like for us all. Not to mention the illnesses that were cascading through the older members of the family. All this fresh off of the heels of the COVID-19 pandemic. It's a wonder I hadn't literally lost my mind. *Or had I?*

This was just the tip of the iceberg. There was so much more going on. People were starting to notice. I would often hear, *"Ebony, slow down," "Ebony you gotta take a break," "Can I help you with anything," "I'm worried about you," or "You can't do it all."* But She thought She could until She couldn't anymore.

Ebony couldn't take being silenced any longer. The whole me had to break free of She. She was taking on too much. She was on the trail to disaster. She was having a breakdown whether she knew it or not.

As often happens, when you get three women who are moms and immensely proud of their children together the conversation turns to our kids. As we talked about how proud we were of the amazing children we'd raised (at this point, they were all on their way out of high school or already attending college). We raved about accolades and accomplishments. We talked about a few challenges we'd encountered, and that is when it happened, I put my proverbial foot in my mouth!

We dove into a conversation that many in our generation have – we talked about how kids in our children's generation are soft and couldn't have made it in our day. We laughed about school being closed because there was less than a half inch of snow on the ground or it was too cold. Being born and raised in Detroit, you are used to the snow, used to the cold. We would have just gotten up early, put on our snow pants, boots, coats, and other winter gear and made the blocks long track to school together. We agreed our kids would not hear of such a thing! We giggled at how we were having our version of our parents "I walked a mile one way up hill to school every morning" conversation. The discussion then turned to how our upbringing taught us how to process our feelings and we were stronger for it. That's when it happened. It was as if I was following instructions that read – open mouth, insert foot when I said, "but did we though? Did we really learn to manage our feelings, or did we just learn to bury them. I think that is why we are all dealing with unhealed trauma and all on somebody's damn therapy couch once a week."

As the last phrase came out of my mouth, I realized I hadn't considered my words before I spoke to them, I just blurted them out because that was how I was really feeling. It was what happened when I didn't let the *professional* version of Ebony be in control. This is what happened when I allowed that little Black girl that wanted so desperately to be a part of the "Black girl crew" to come out. I'd made the situation awkward. Tears were now streaming down Tasha's face. *How could I have forgotten that she'd just returned to work from a stress leave? How could I have been so insensitive? How would I overcome this one?* I was immensely sorry, and very well intentioned. Then panic set in. *I knew that being in the position of most senior leader in the area, I'd put the company at risk, my job at risk, what was I going to do?* I had what seemed like a million simultaneous thoughts in a split second. Imagine a beautiful mind type scene internally with a little Black girl magic sprinkled on it. In a split second I had a thousand thoughts racing through my mind. I was playing back scenes from previous interactions at warp speed, remembering people who had made one wrong move or made a careless statement and their careers were ended, I was mapping out thousands of thoughts on the wall of my mind, numbers were whirling as I attempted to break the code of how I would continue on in my role – what would I say, how could I fix this. While I didn't see people that weren't there, the thoughts were coming unbelievably fast, almost at paralyzing speed. I'd created and lived in a world where I could not make a mistake and that was about to break me.

Finally (or really like two seconds later), I took a deep breath and decided, *forget the company and the job. Right now, I just hurt my sister (or so I thought), and I need to tend to her feelings.* I asked her to walk with me. As we took a walk together and I apologized, she told me there was no need to apologize. She told me that I was exactly right. She told me that my comment had reminded her of what she was working through in therapy, but I was exactly right. We were all in therapy because we'd not learned to manage our emotions and our trauma but instead had learned to bury it. She shared that she agreed with a thought I had – instead of being in therapy as adults, to learn the mental and emotional tools we needed to survive, we should break the cycle and make sure that our kids are in therapy from childhood, so they don't have the mental and emotional scars we have. We've taught them to care for their bodies by getting regular physicals, their eyes by getting regular eye exams, their teeth by getting regular dental cleanings, and as we get older, we add on the mammograms, the colonoscopies and all the other regular tests. Therapy should be no different. We embraced and, in that moment, we were two strong Black women that were not invisible, we saw each other. I'd given her permission to feel what she was feeling right in the spot she felt it, and she'd given me permission to do the same. In that moment, I decided I'd been away from therapy too long and made an appointment to return.

The first step to breaking through and getting better was admitting there was an issue, being okay with it and creating a plan to get better. I knew that I had to get myself in some therapy. While I'd been in therapy before, this time was different because it was not just me feeling a little sad and like I wanted to talk to someone. Even my primary care doctor was referring me to engage in some type of behavioral health program. This was worse than any time before. Worse than when I was having frequent panic attacks trying to finish a degree, worse than when I was overwhelmed with being a new mom and trying to figure out life as a wife and mother, worse than when I'd lost loved ones and needed grief counseling. This time I was spiraling. I was losing control, and I knew it was time to do the work— work that I'd avoided for far too long.

So, they say knowing is half the battle. Well, I can tell you that ain't true. I had a long battle ahead of me. Just knowing I had an anxiety disorder and was suffering from severe depression was not half the battle. I was having a breakdown. I know that is not a clinical term and isn't utilized in the medical field or study of mental and emotional health, but I want to call it like I see it...I was having a freaking breakdown. I had to make peace with it. I had to do something about it. I had to figure out how to deal with it. They say knowing is half the battle. I say knowing is the start of the battle.

First up, reconciling whether or not to tell people what I was dealing with. While there is a movement to make caring for your mental health more acceptable in the Black community, in the corporate community and in the world at large, we simply aren't there yet from an acceptance perspective. And baby, let me tell you, as the daughter of two preachers, the world expects my prayer life to be strong enough to get through this stuff. Or at least that is what I believed people would think. I also thought that the work world would just think She was trying to get some time off because everyone was on "stress leave" and it wasn't looked so highly upon. Plus, this is Dr. Stone—she raised kids, worked, and completed a doctoral degree at the same time. If that didn't break her, what would. Did my friends and family really need to know? How incredibly weak would they think I was? So much to reconcile. And then there was the overachieving perfectionist that She was, that kept sneaking in to ask her, *if you take this time off, what will you accomplish - can you finish that book, finally launch the podcast, start coaching and writing again?* I literally spent a week trying to make it make sense.

I knew four people for sure that I could trust with my truth. They would think no differently of me for knowing my truth, they would encourage me, and they would help me to heal— my husband of twenty-two years who saw the wheels falling off, my mom who was often the voice telling me to slow down, my younger brother who was always in support of me and had also helped me through a mini meltdown just six months prior when I showed up at his house on a Saturday a blubbering mess, and my best friend who was a psychologist herself. So, I told them all. They all were supportive and told me basically it was about time. As for my kids, they had enough going on, I didn't want to worry them so I simply told them I was taking a few weeks off.

I had to tell the people at work something. *Or did I.* According to Mr. Stone, I didn't owe them a damn thing, but it surely felt wrong. She decided it was in fact wrong, so She came up with a plan. She'd go into work on Monday, tell her boss what was going on, meet with her direct reports on Tuesday, and then prepare to leave the following Monday, the 4th of September. It was settled. She sent the following text messages to her therapist late Friday evening:

Hi. I'm feeling so guilty about leaving like this. You were right, about me needing time to process it.

Leaving like this is stressing me. If I leave after this week that gives me time to tell my team the right way and my boss the right way.

Can we make the leave start on the 4th? I want to take care of myself. I need to take care of myself. But I can't do it and not be organized when I leave. I need to get things in order and I want to be fair.

I'll talk to my boss Monday and my team in our Tuesday morning meeting. It's only fair. I care too much about my team. Is that okay? I'm on schedules to speak and everything and it just feels wrong to drop them like that. But I know I gotta do it. Just one more week.

I didn't get a response. But it was Friday evening and the therapist needed time to step away, too. I later found out that she was in session and that is why she didn't respond right away. I was beginning to come unwound. My mind was racing a hundred miles a minute with thoughts of things I'd heard said about people on stress leave, of my uncle who had schizophrenia, of my dad and grandma who both died of dementia. *Was my brain going on me? Was it mental? Was it neurological? Was I literally losing my mind?*

The next day I tried to focus on my son's bowling tournament. I was there physically, but mentally I was in fifty thousand different places. I was worrying about other people. *Would my assistant be okay while I was gone, would they take her from me. I really liked her; I didn't want to start all over with a new assistant. What about the one other girl that reported to me? She was a Black woman and so very talented. I wanted her to be seen.* I knew the guys would be okay. They were liked and had great reputations. *What about my peer? How could I just walk away and not tell him anything? We trusted each other with all kinds of stuff.* My mind literally raced like this for hours until I was exhausted and in tears.

Sunday morning, I woke up still very saddened. I was extremely late to church because I spent the morning crying. I cried through church. I cried after church. The sermon my mom preached that week was entitled *Having a Heart Like Mary in a World Like Marth* and was about being like Mary, not missing out on life because you are busying yourself like Martha. I knew God meant the sermon for me, but I couldn't figure out how to apply it at that moment. All I could do was cry. Literally all day.

I think Ebony and the version of Ebony everyone else saw, the one I called "She" were in a battle inside of me. She needed to go out on leave the proper and polite way. Ebony just needed to leave. Lucky for me, for the first time in decades Ebony won. I texted my therapist again and told her I'd changed my mind and Monday was just fine because I needed to take care of myself. Then I hurried and sent this text that She carefully drafted to my boss. Drafting the text message was *She's* consolation prize for losing the battle, She would still get to say it properly so as not to ruffle any feathers.

Good Evening –
I am writing concerning my current situation. As you know, for the past couple of years, I've been dealing with some health concerns.

What I have not shared is that over the last 6-9 months it's been discovered a few other issues exist and that treatment for these issues have caused the need for me to take more drastic action to increase my overall health.

Last week I was either in person or virtually meeting with health professionals at least 4 times. My care team has removed me from work for at least 6 weeks (to be evaluated after the 6-week recovery). I'd originally asked that they not do it immediately and give me time (at least a week) to speak with you and my team.

However, over this weekend, as things got progressively worse, I made the decision to put myself first, so I will be out on leave following the recommendations of my health team starting Monday.

In processing everything I've needed to process this week, I am not yet ready to discuss my diagnoses with anyone other than my immediate family. My team is in really good shape - Andrew and Robert both have offered to help with Stacey in the past so I will be asking Andrew to lead Stacey and Shawn in my absence.

Brenda will continue to support Stacey's team as she's been doing, support Andrew in Tina's absence, work on the projects I've assigned her and possibly help support Robert temporarily as Ashley may be moving to a different role. I will send them a similar email as well as my peer David. Thank you in advance for understanding.

I freaked out, cut the phone off, and cried myself to sleep.

In the morning, through tears, I cut the phone back on, read her response, in which she requested that I copy her on any emails I sent to my team. She'd tried to reach me through multiple means, but I'd purposely shut them all down while I cried myself to sleep. I complied with the request of my boss by sending emails to each of my team members and copying her on the emails.

I must say that her response and those of my direct reports was caring, filled with concern and compassion. They were concerned about me, too. No matter how well-crafted She thought the email was, they knew something was wrong.

It was done. I was on leave and now knowing was the beginning of my journey.

It was the last week of August. Kids were headed back to school, school buses were back on the road, rush hour traffic was a thing again, homework would be a staple, packing lunches was a necessity, uniforms needed to be cleaned and pressed, and all the things that kicked off the "beginning of the year" for many families were in full bloom. I usually look forward to this time of the year. As a planner at heart, a strategist at work, and someone that literally longed for structure, this time of year meant the return of routine. Unlike the beginning of summer that lent itself to the weather I enjoyed, but usually sent my family into "anything goes mode," fall typically meant I could get back on track, but this year was different.

My daughter was away at school, learning to be an adult (with the safety net of a college campus). My oldest child had moved out on his own and hadn't asked for any assistance (aside from utilizing my vehicle for longer than I'd expected), and the baby boy was now a sophomore, coming into his own. Not to mention,

I'd yielded responsibility of the morning *get ready for school* ritual to my husband late in the former school year. I had nowhere to go, I had nothing to do. My calendar at work was probably cleared at this point and all I had on my personal calendar was my first therapy session since the leave started. I wish I could say I stayed in bed until that session because I was resting. That isn't it, though. I stayed in bed until that session because I was sad. I was really sad. I was depressed and in a major way.

Prior to this experience, I'd been sad before. At some points in my life for weeks at a time. I chalked that up to things like the seasons changing, a loved one dealing with a chronic illness, or life just lifin.' Unfortunately, all that did was cause me to bury Ebony deeper and allow *She* to continue to develop. It didn't allow the discovery of my anxiety and depression. It also didn't allow me to develop the necessary tools to manage either. This time She was trying to pull it together and I was beating her down. I know now that that was the best thing for me, but during the battle, I literally felt like I was losing my mind. She wanted to get out of the bed, but I couldn't. She wanted to just shake it off and be happy, but I couldn't. She wanted to see this as a break filled with goals that needed to be accomplished, but I couldn't. She wanted to cancel the therapy session, but I couldn't.

To be honest, I don't remember a lot about the words of that first therapy session, but I remember the feelings that were evoked before, during, and after the session. Before the session, there was this overwhelming fear, I was petrified really. See, I grew up with an uncle that was schizophrenic. *Had I developed a severe mental condition that would change the course of my life? What had She done to her career, would it ever be the same?* Before the session, she felt so guilty, *how could she abandon the people at work she had truly come to care about and those that she didn't really care for but had committed to?* I was sad, really sad; confused and scared.

During the session, my emotions were all over the place. A virtual patchwork quilt of emotion. I was mad. I was sad. I was confused. I was scared. I was curious. I felt overwhelmed and dejected. Yet, I was somehow relieved, appreciative of being in the space where I could bear it all without judgment or ramification. If you can name an emotion, I probably felt it in that one-hour session. I talked through tears the entire time. I believe I mostly talked about work. I was so focused on work; I don't even think I talked about me at all. I was very much concerned about all things work related. I would later get to see some of the therapy notes as a part of my leave claim and words like disheveled, cluttered, and unkempt were used to describe me and my surroundings and those descriptors were very true. I don't remember the exact words and phrases I uttered during the session, but one thing I knew for sure was I was a complete mess during the session. I have no idea how my therapist made sense of anything during that session and several to follow.

I remember sharing my feelings with the therapist and her telling me to stop being so hard on myself, that I would be proud of choosing me for the first time in a very long time, if ever. I remember thinking during that session, there is no way I will feel better in six weeks. I think the more I talked and the more she talked to me, the worse I felt. I felt like there was a war unfolding inside of me. There were things buried deep inside that I had to come face to face with. I had to admit to feelings that made me very uncomfortable. I was deploying a strategy different than I ever had before. Simple honesty of emotion. I prided myself on being honest, but to exist in the world I was in, I often had to deny the emotions and deploy my truth in a tactical fashion considering the feelings of all involved, carefully crafting each sentence with well-placed words, as to not offend, not come off as the angry Black woman and worst of all not be seen by my own as a sellout. But in therapy, in these sessions, I had to be raw unadulterated Ebony.

A co-worker of mine once said to me, "I can't wait until everyone gets unedited, unfiltered, raw Dr. Stone – the one not handcuffed by the rules of the environment in which she exists." Well, what he didn't know was that the road to unedited, unfiltered, and raw Dr. Stone was paved with cement blocks that had been mixed with the tears I would shed in these sessions.

I remember thinking, "I have heard celebrities and everyday people alike say you've gotta do the hard work." Well, if this was the beginning of the work, they had not chosen the right word as a descriptor. This work was not hard, I did hard; this work was terrifying. I know hard when I see it. In fact, I once had a very good friend say to me (about a difficult situation), "Ebby, you do hard things, you are a whole doctor, you just haven't really decided it's time to do it so you haven't". My husband told me, "Anytime you decide to do something, and you really put your mind to it, you do it no matter how hard it is...it's when you haven't really convinced yourself you can or that it's time, that you don't." Like many of you reading these pages, I was known for doing hard things. This was not hard, this was not difficult, at this point in my emotional journey this work was unfathomable. This work required a modern-day miracle. This was work that only God himself would be able to see me through.

After the session, I felt worse. I LOVED my therapist, still do to this day and I am grateful that God used her in my life. Talking to my therapist felt like talking to a trusted friend, and wise advisor, someone you could tell your secrets to and they would go to the grave. Having to say the words, express the feelings, allow my inner self to peak out was scary though. I had to start to admit all of the things that I've never admitted to anyone. I had to actually talk about being a Black woman in corporate America, the hurt and the pain that I'd hidden for so long in an effort to be a light for others and to travel the road I thought I was destined to remain on. I had to talk about the devastating feelings caused by those I wanted so desperately to call my sister. I had to admit that I no longer gave a damn about any of the work that was in front of me (with the exception of the mentoring and coaching that was inherent to my position). I had to actually talk about the insecurities I had as a wife and mother. I had to address the feelings of failing my dad during his illness because I was not strong enough to handle what the disease did to his mind. I had to address the areas in my marriage that weren't picture perfect. I had to do the work.

I've always had a really great support system. While I was sad, I was busy trying not to allow myself to feel the emotion like I normally did, my support system was happy. Not happy that I was sad, depressed, or even confused about next steps. What they were happy about was that something, no matter what that something was, had caused me to stop, to take a break, to face the reality of my life. To pause.

Chapter Eight

PATH TOWARD COMPLETE HEALING

Almost a month in and it is time to follow up with my primary care physician. I'd be nervous no matter what, but to make matters worse, I'd changed primary care physicians to utilize a physician group dedicated to only those employed by my employer. When I made the move, I cited convenience, supporting the organization, and the high level of client service that I knew would be required to be a part of the organization. The dedicated discounted Walgreens pharmacy was just icing on the cake. I didn't allow myself to do the usual "separation of church and state." I mean, I carried a separate "work" cell phone, didn't hang out with many folks from work, and did my best to only make after work "appearances" only when necessary. But I'd let my guard down and made the change, it was after all what the executives in the organization were doing.

I was anxious for a number of reasons. First, I had to go on to the campus. That is how referred to the number of office buildings, high rises, and parking structures the organization owned in the downtown area we worked in. Many of its companies were located there. I was going into the nucleus for my doctor's appointment. If it is possible to feel your blood pressure rise, I felt it. I was frightened of running into someone I knew and having to explain why I looked perfectly fine but was on leave. Secondly, I needed to tell my doctor how I was feeling. The fact that things weren't getting better fast enough, and I'd refused to take the medicine he'd prescribed was bound to be an uncomfortable conversation.

Before I get into what happened during that appointment, let me tell you what the last four weeks of my leave consisted of. For the first four weeks I tried to get over the crying spells, I tried to utilize my time wisely, I tried to determine how to continue to be there for others, I tried to think of and research business ideas, I tried to put on a good face for others, I tried...She tried. But it didn't work. I'd literally not done much of anything. I laid in the bed thinking about what I needed to do, wondering when I would come out of this and how things would look when I do. She tried to show up countless times, but I was pretty sure She was the reason I was in this mess, and I wasn't allowing her to take over anymore.

For four weeks, I'd felt like I was the main character in a Spike Lee movie when they realized what was happening. That moment when they are not frozen, they can move but it is if they aren't there. They are seeing everything move around them, may even know what they need to do but they are powerless to do anything other than stand there and watch. That was me, the main character in my life, watching and knowing what needed to happen (or so I thought) and powerless to do anything about it.

My brother had checked on me the weekend before and asked if I was getting any rest at all. I described the feeling to him. I told him I was the main character in my own Spike Lee movie just watching the world go by, waiting on a chance to get back in the action and trying to determine what that should look like. I told him if nothing else, I was at least not doing much. Not sure if it was really rest and relaxation, but it was something. I couldn't have prepared for his response. It was jarring but needed. He always spoke to me in love and that is the same thing he did that day.

"They call that like an existential crisis, right?" he requested.

What the hell, am I in a crisis? I'm not in a crisis, I am just a little sad, a little stressed, a little anxious, or was I? I wasn't sure. I thought I was losing my mind but could others really tell? Were they noticing my crisis? I wasn't even sure how to respond, but I did.

"Hummm, not sure. I gotta look that up. I am not sure what that means. I am going to have to do some research," I said.

I honestly wasn't sure what existential meant, what I did know was that any type of crisis was not something I was willing to admit to at that moment. These words kept hitting me like punches. Every time there was a new one, I couldn't handle it. I didn't know where to put it, how to process it, or what to do with it.

I tucked it away and of course looked it up later. *If I was in a crisis, did I really need the medication? Not sure. Nope, not doing it, I don't need another pill.* I had an appointment with the therapist that same afternoon and maybe I would ask her if I was in crisis mode. As luck would have it, there was no need to ask her. The conversation itself proved that I was in some type of emotional crisis, no matter what it was called. What seemed to start off as small talk about music at the beginning of a therapy session uncovered a slew of emotions.

"Oh wow, he loves music like that? Do you all own a record player?" the therapist asked.

I could no longer hold back the tears. We had a record player. One that had been gifted to my youngest son from my mom, as a keepsake. It was my dad's. He'd been gone for six years, but it felt like it was just yesterday. For the first time I was able to say out loud things that I'd never admitted before. It was beyond hurtful to see my biggest cheerleader slip away slowly to a disease that robbed us of our loved one before his physical body was gone… dementia. Daddy always had something positive to say to cheer you on. "You know I tried not to like that boy, but you got you a good one there in that husband of yours," or "y'all are doing a great job raising those kids,"or "oooooo weeeeee, you got you a big ole pretty house," or "you just smart as a whip," etc. I was daddy's little girl; his pride and joy.

I'll never forget that day in church. I am sure that many people judged me because I stayed away from church for a very long time after that painful day, but that was between me and my God. He knew why. Let me explain. I went to church and sat in the section to the right of the pulpit in our small but mighty sanctuary. As the announcements ended and the clerk asked for any visitors to stand, my dad rose to thank them all for coming as he always did. Daddy was a prominent figure, so when he stood, everyone noticed. He was 6'3" with a smile that could light up any room and a voice that commanded attention. On that day, his voice commanded attention alright as he bellowed toward the side of the sanctuary I was sitting on. "Good morning young lady, where are you visiting us from?" As congregants we were all confused because there were no visitors sitting in that section, we'd all been members of the church for years. "You, in the flowered shirt." *Me? Was my daddy talking about me? Did he not know who I was? Was this the disease?* Yep, that was it— that was the disease— at that moment he didn't know me. Because of the reactions of people around, he realized he should have known me. Daddy and I were both good at navigating situations, reading rooms, and easing out of uncomfortable situations. He and I both laughed it off, made some random lighthearted jokes and moved on. Daddy was gonna have to come out of the pulpit. The disease was progressing, and things only got worse from there.

When the disease progressed to a stage that Mom could no longer keep him at home and he had to be moved into a nursing home, emotions were high. There was an altercation in the family, fueled by years of unresolved and undiscussed hurt, from the heightened emotion of having to make that decision no one wanted to make. It formed a wedge between a few family members that still exists to this day. A wedge that places me in the middle of a very slippery slope. I simply couldn't see my daddy— my hero— in that condition. It simply devastated me. I didn't visit much because I just couldn't handle it. I threw myself deeper into work and caring for my kids. *Was that the wrong thing...sure felt like it.* I felt an insurmountable amount of guilt around that decision because I know if it was me, Daddy would have been right by my side every day. The whole therapy session was spent talking through that situation. It felt good to admit it, and I had to forgive myself. I did what I thought I needed to do to hold it together for me and my family and Daddy would definitely understand that.

Daddy did understand because he told me in his own way

before he became non-verbal. I went to visit on one of my monthly visits because that was all I could muster. He looked up at me, got a great big smile on his face and said, "Hey, I know that lady right there!" He gave me a big hug, my kids and I took a picture with Paw-paw (as they called him), and I knew he knew me. I'd been holding this in so long, it felt good to get it out, but that was just the beginning. My therapist was right, I needed to do something with that grief...I needed to somehow memorialize Daddy. Maybe a day of family golf every year (one of his favorite things), or a day on the grill (another one of his favorite things) and a balloon release, maybe a basketball tournament (another favorite) to raise funds for a cause. I don't know what it will be, but it will be something. I felt better. In that one moment, I conquered one thing. I didn't let the things that She would have typically pulled together to show her strength and composure come out. I'd let the whole me show up. I was proud and a bit relieved.

What other things had I buried that needed to come out? I know there is a lot and in four weeks, I'd only gotten to one! Could I really tell my physician that after four weeks I'd done two things. Talked about my dad in one session that made me feel a lot better and went to see my baby girl for family day, which also put a smile on my face. *Was that all that I'd managed to accomplish in four weeks?* I didn't take the medicine he gave me and Daddy always said, "did you take the advice I already gave you? If not, don't come in here asking for more advice, come ask for more advice when the advice I gave you doesn't work." Now I had to go face the music, I hadn't taken the advice...

I could prepare for that. What I couldn't prepare for was what I'd do if I saw someone I worked with. I drove to the appointment in complete silence terrified the entire way. *Why didn't I make this appointment on a Monday or Friday when everyone works from home? Why didn't I ask someone to drop me off at the front door so I could scurry in and scurry back out minimizing the chance of anyone seeing me? Why didn't I just try to see if I could do this as a virtual appointment?* I was not okay with this. I parked in the back, tried to slide in the back door but it was out of service. I quickly moved to the front door, but my badge wouldn't work because I was on leave. I had to wait in line to get a visitor's badge. When I finally got it in hand, I ran upstairs and prayed the entire time that no one would see me. I didn't want to explain.

The appointment went as planned, except this time, I left really considering taking the medication. I didn't want to feel this way any longer. I needed myself back. Luckily, I didn't run into anyone and got out of there with just a $17 parking bill.

On my way back home, my phone rang.

"Hey, what up?" It was my brother. That was our unique greeting, no 's' on 'what.'

"Nothing much, what up?" I answered.

"You downtown?" he asked.

"Yeah, I had a doctor's appointment, how did you know?"

He responded, "Chris just came to my desk and said, 'I just saw your sister' and I told her I don't even think my sister is in the state and she said, 'she is because I just saw her.'"

I'd narrowly escaped seeing anyone, but they'd laid eyes on me. *Damn! Oh well!!* As a well-known executive, a Black female executive that most people knew just because there weren't many of us, I didn't have the privacy I desired to deal with my current mental state. I had to ask myself though, why did I need privacy? Why couldn't I boldly proclaim that I was dealing with depression and anxiety and needed time off to heal just like people proclaimed they'd had babies or knee surgery, or dialysis— it all required treatment, and all should be treated the same, shouldn't it? Why was I hiding?

The doctor's appointment went as expected and the doctor understood my hesitation. But it was starting to set in that I was going to have to come face to face in my everyday life with what I'd experienced. While I knew it was no one's business I was feeling like I would not be able to keep this a secret.

Since I knew I would not be able to keep this whole experience a secret, I did what I always did to feel better. I started to write. Writing has always been cathartic for me. As a little girl, when I'd get in trouble or want to express some big emotion that I had problems expressing, I'd write. I'd write in my journal, I'd write letters to my parents, or I'd even take a stab at writing poetry. I express myself in a few ways and writing is at the top of the list. As I started to put words to paper, I realized that what I had to say about my experience needed to be shared. It needed to be shared so that I could start to heal, but also so that others could heal. I was going through this experience writing about it and God was going to allow a book to come out on the other end. I'd been working on another book, that hopefully God will see fit to release at a later date, but I realized that this book had to be written for me and the thousands of women like me experiencing this sense of spiraling out of control.

Chapter Nine

THE HEALING JOURNEY

August 27th … for all my life that date was just my cousin's birthday. We were grown, so that day just meant to send him a quick text to say, "Happy Birthday." This past August 27th started off the same way, but it would not end that way. That was the day I chose me late that evening and decided that I had to listen to my therapist and pause. It was now emblazoned on my mind as the day that things had to change. I've tried to figure out why that day was the day. I can't tell you why, there is nothing special about it. It is just the day that I chose me. It meant that I would return to work on October 9th after a six-week pause.

A pause, a hard reset, what did that mean? Reset? Rest? Rest - REST - what did rest mean? It wasn't something I was familiar with, and it felt foreign. One of my very first assignments in therapy was to create an acronym for REST to remind me of what it meant. I prayed that the words would come to me. While I don't claim to hear the audible voice of God, I do feel led by His spirit and I was led to the following: Release and Restore; Ebony First; Sacrifice (rest is a sacrifice); and Test (you will be tested). Is that what rest was? I was confused, but at that point in my journey I was so out of sorts that I was ready to push on and try anything to feel better. I was prepared to release and be restored. So, I put myself first. I'd sacrifice things that I felt had to be done to rest, and I would remember that tests will come— I will pass some and I will fail some, but I will continue to try.

I'd be lying if I said those six weeks were easy, they were not. I wrote the following in my journal so I could make sure to share with my therapist because I was still in documentation mode. I still felt like I needed to justify caring for myself. *What if someone asked what I did, how I felt and called me to the carpet to justify this stress leave I was on.* I'd sat in meetings about other people on stress leave, so I needed to make sure that my leave was justified and that no one thought I was just trying to get time off of work.

8/28 - Cried all day.
8/29 - Woke up crying again.
8/30 - First appointment.
9/2 - Waiting all day.
9/4 - At least I could hear the smile in baby girl's voice when she called.

9/5 - It doesn't always take faith to grind, but it often takes faith to stop grinding. Rest is not a response to fatigue. If that is the only time you stop, you missed some things, God didn't stop because he was tired, he stopped because he was accomplished. If we don't stop because of what we accomplish, we will end up like Elijah. Taking Emory to school. 3 sermons, a bee sting, scholarship apps, band parent meeting. Where is the rest? Where is the time for me?
9/6 - He said, "she's just laying around not doing anything."
9/9 - I need to take care of me for just a little while.
9/10 - We need to increase income by at least 25%. Seeing people from work - why is that a problem?
9/13 - Three pieces of bacon, Niya is doing better, business attire, the list.
9/20 - Thursday felt overwhelming and I fought tears.
9/21 - Paralyzed - I feel like I am faking my way to better like always, I am not getting better, I am just doing the same thing, putting on the same masks. I'm faking it!
9/25 - I'm a mess, we can't get on the same page about finances.

At each appointment, I spoke to my therapist about these notes that I would hastily jot down to make sure I could remember what I needed to talk about. I honestly felt like I needed to justify it to her as well, I felt like I had to justify everything. "Ebony, you are not ready to return to work. You are just starting to disconnect from day-to-day work. You need at least another 6 weeks to start to heal and make decisions about your next steps." And just like that, the leave was extended. The short-term disability administrator requested a form from my therapist, she returned it, and it was approved instantly. November 20th was the new return to work date.

THE FIRST GOOD DAY

October 3rd was a really good day. I was at peace. I found myself smiling. I didn't do anything special. The sun was shining. The birds were chirping. I checked on the garden, sat outside with the dog, stopped by moms, and picked the youngest up from school. The house was a mess, but I left it as it was. The bills needed to be paid, but nothing was behind, so that, too, could wait. I just existed. *Is this what rest really felt like? Why did I ask that question because the answer was yes.* My acronym for rest was playing out. I was releasing things for the purpose of restoration, I was choosing Ebony, I was sacrificing. But it didn't hit me that there had not been a test yet and boy was it on its way.

As I lay in bed explaining to my husband that for the first time in a long time I felt really good for that day. I was ready to do the work to make this my normal. *This is what life is supposed to be like, right?* Of course there will be challenges, but for the most part, life is supposed to be full of peace, learning, evolving, experiencing joy, and overcoming the tests as they come your way, right?

> 10:10 p.m., text alert: I glanced down, and it was my cousin, Tonya, who lived in Atlanta. *She probably has a question about the family reunion. I'll check*

> *and respond in a sec, when we finish this conversation … a conversation that is going great, again, for the first time in a long time.*
>
> 10:11p.m., text alert: I glanced down. It was my girlfriend, Shay. She texts a lot. *I'll check it and respond in just a sec. Probably something about bowling this week or her upcoming 50th.*
>
> 10:11p.m., text alert: I glanced down. It was Natasha, another freshman parent from the university my daughter attended.

Everyone knows that by 10:00 on a normal night I am in bed, why was I receiving so many text messages back-to-back. I snatched the phone up, mostly out of frustration and with plans to put it on silent mode, but figured I'd better look at Natasha's message. It read, *You ok? Our girls are ok. We are speeding up the highway trying to get to the campus.* My heart started racing, my mouth got dry, a million thoughts ran through my head. As I read the text to my husband, I simultaneously texted back these words, *I think I am okay, what's going on? Did I miss something?*

The phone rang, it was Natasha. While she was telling me what was happening, I was flipping to my cousin's text message. My cousin, Tanya, used to live in the area where my daughter attended school and was there on business, so she still got text alerts about things going on in the area. Her message read *Cuz!! Call and check on your daughter. I'm in the area working and just got an alert on my phone that six people got shot at her university.* Natasha was explaining that she was on her way, she'd talked to our daughters, they were safe in my daughter's room on lock down, and she would call when she got to campus and if need be take my child along with hers away from campus.

I hung up the phone and the tears started running. My baby girl was almost nine hours away from me, living away from home for the first time, and now she was on lockdown. I called her and she didn't answer. I called again, no answer. I texted her *Call me now!* The phone rang, it was her.

"Baby, are you okay?"

"Yes, Mommy I am okay. I am in my room."

"What is all of that that I hear? What happened?"

"That is my roommate and her friends. I don't know exactly what happened, I was doing hair in my room, and people started coming in saying they were shooting in the cafe. Oh Mommy, that is the girl whose hair I was doing, she had just left, I need to see if she is okay, I will call you right back," and she hung up.

She didn't call right back, so I called her. "You didn't call me back. Why didn't you call me and tell me what was going on babe? Where is Mikayla? Is the door locked?"

"Mommy, I am fine, Mikayla is in here, too, and yes the door is locked."

"How many of you are in there? Where are your suitemates? Can you move the closet in front of the door so no one can get in?"

"There are about 8 of us in here. We are fine, but I have to get off of the phone because they told us to cut the lights out and to be quiet."

"Baby, respond to my text messages."

"Okay," and she hung up.

I literally stayed glued to the television watching the news coverage, I scoured social media for updates. I constantly checked my parent groups. I talked to Natasha because she was there and I was nine hours away! I called my other cousin who lived there in the area as well to make sure she could get to my baby girl if need be and she assured me that once there was the all clear, she would go and get baby girl if things weren't safe, but right now she couldn't get anywhere close to campus. Late that night, they were able to give the all clear. My daughter went to her cousin's and by the next morning, I sent a plane ticket for her to come home. I needed to lay eyes on her and hug her.

My first day of feeling good was marred by this heinous act and I'd failed the test. My baby girl told me she was okay and in retrospect I understood why she hadn't called me. She was okay, but she knew I'd worry and I'd go into panic mode, passing my anxiety along to any willing participant and she didn't want to participate. She knew if she called, I'd go into hyper overdrive asking ten thousand questions, and that is exactly what I did. It was painfully obvious I was at the very beginning of the work I had to do. Yes, that was a stressful situation, and any parent would be worried, but when I look at how everyone else around me was able to handle it, including my husband, and the fact that in that type of situation, my daughter was concerned with not worrying me more than she was of informing me, I knew what I had to do. I was ready. I had about six weeks to get it all in order and I went to work.

THE FIRST EXTENSION

During the weeks to come, I was focused on being present. I was determined not to interact with work at all, at the advice of my therapist but also because I needed to shut off as much of the outside world as I could to heal. I was only going to interact with things that I had to in my personal life. I wanted to do things that were important to me. Things that I kept buried because I didn't have time to explore them, like write. I'd been working on a book for a while. I had a whiteboard full of sticky notes with chapter titles and what they would be about. I'd outlined the lessons I'd learned as a Black woman in corporate America and how to overcome the unique obstacles that we come up against. I'd spent more than two decades building a stellar career and I wanted to share that with the generations behind me. I had some keynote speeches on my mind that I hadn't had the time to cultivate or put together the slide decks for and I wanted to have them ready just in case. I wanted to clean and organize my house from top to bottom. I could check off all of the things that I'd been neglecting, and I could do it on my time while I rested.

When I sat down to work on the book, two things happened. I felt in my spirit that it wasn't time for that book, but it was time for another. God was leading me to write about my experience in caring for my mental health. You are reading the obedience of that guidance now. The more I wrote about my experience, the more I came across and interacted with people who would share with me that they were having similar experiences. I'd share that I was writing about it and every time, I'd get a response something like, "I am so glad you are going to share, it is a story that needs to be told. You telling your story will give others permission to take care of themselves and know that they are not alone," so I continued to write.

One day, I'd picked my youngest son up from school, something I'd been able to do every day that year for the very first time in his entire life. As we drove down the freeway, it happened. My heart started to race from nowhere. I felt like I'd run a marathon, and I was just driving the ten minutes to and from his school. The sweat started to trickle down my face. I didn't want to worry him, and I was approaching our exit, which led right into our subdivision. I pushed the button to crack the window, took a deep breath, and just dealt with it for the two minutes or so it took us to arrive at home from that moment. I told him to go let the dog out. I let the window down and laid the seat back in the car. They were back. The anxiety attacks I had when I was in my last semester of undergraduate school and working forty hours a week, taking eighteen credits, and still living in the dorms. The attacks always happened when I was seemingly doing nothing. They never happened while I was in overdrive. Only when I thought I was resting. I realized that I needed to tell my therapist and physician about this, and this time find tools to work through them.

My therapist was not surprised by these attacks I had started to experience and told me that it was perfectly normal to experience them when seemingly nothing was going on. Through my work with her, I realized that though I made progress, I wasn't sure that I was ready to return to the grind of an executive role. I realized that I didn't love the role I was in. It was not the organization, it was not the people, it was not the work. The organization had promise. Although it was not without challenge it would continue to be a force to be reckoned with and a place where many would love to be employed. It was not the people. I'd met some of the most amazing people I'd ever met in my life in that place (and some of the worst) and many of them loved and respected me more than people I'd known for most of my life. It was not the work. The work was important and was in many ways disruptive to an industry that had been stagnated for far too long. It was me;

I'd started to unearth an Ebony that had been buried for far too long and I didn't want to re-bury her by doing work I didn't love. I wanted to push into my passion. I wanted to write. I wanted to speak. I wanted to teach. I wanted to help other Black women in the workplace lean into their full selves and climb the corporate ladder or reach their other dreams.

Thoughts of shifting gears for the next phase of my journey started to enter my mind. My youngest son was loving the access to me that he had for the first time, and honestly, I was enjoying doing things like just simply being able to take him to pick up his band sweater – gave me more joy than any project I'd worked on professionally in a long time. I remember looking at my son and wondering if he felt the same, so I asked him. "Hey, would you prefer I continue to work at home, or do you think I should go back to the office?" To which he responded, "Mommy, I definitely think you should stay home, but not for us, for you! You're not as stressed as you are when you have to go in to work. It's fun with you home. Can we stop and get me something to eat?" Yep, he moved right on to food, he is a fifteen-year-old boy and that is what they think about all day and all night (among a few other adolescent thoughts). But the reality was, he was right. I had calmed down, but so had my entire family. We were all benefiting from the work I was doing on myself, and I was even enjoying myself more. The Ebony that had been buried through the years of just trying to be what everyone thought she should be, was emerging.

I was slowly realizing what I needed to do. I had two really big decisions to make. As I reflected and healed, I realized that I had to take responsibility for where I was. While it would be easy to say that the corporate environment was solely responsible for my current state of mind, that wasn't true. It would be easy to say that my family responsibilities are unrealistic and are solely responsible for my current state of mind, but that wasn't true. It would be easy to say that any of the things that were a part of my life were solely responsible or that the combination was the reason. The reason was me. She had buried Ebony for far too long. She wasn't all bad though, she'd helped me create a series of rules that had served me well in my career, for decades. The rules were great for my protection, for my growth if followed properly. I needed to get back to those rules in a different context.

MY RULES

One of the things that I'd done well my entire life was set standards and live by a certain set of rules. When I was a child, I lived by my parents' rules and there were a lot of them, but they kept me on the right track. When I was in college (undergraduate and graduate school) I devised a system and a set of rules that served me well and allowed me to execute at a high level when I put my mind to it—after two years of partying hard, but that's a story for a different book. From holding eighteen credits and working a full-time job in my last semester of undergraduate school to completing an entire doctoral program while raising three kids, being married, and working on climbing the corporate ladder complete with a 205-page dissertation, when I applied my rules, I fared well at execution. I now just needed to make sure I applied these rules as the full Ebony not Ebony's representative – She.

When I started my corporate journey, I set my sights high. I knew that I wanted to be an executive in the corporate world. I couldn't tell you what I wanted to be working on in that executive world, but I knew I wanted to be the Black girl in the corner office. I wanted to adorn the classy, sassy business suits with the shoes that were to die for. I remember the first business suit I owned. It was a black on black, pinstripe, double breasted pants suit that I wore with a pair of black patent leather pumps with an exposed arch. My mom bought that one and a beige one with pearl buttons. I loved the part of me I was able to muster up when I put those suits on. I remember pacing back and forth in front of the mirror in my room and delivering fake speeches, imagining staff meetings, and admiring myself in the mirror. Whatever that feeling I had when I was in the mirror, was the feeling I wanted to have daily.

I also knew that I wanted to explore some entrepreneurial ventures including those in real estate and helping other Black women. The details I didn't have worked out because I was only twenty-two-years-old, but I had a general idea of what that journey looked like when I saw entrepreneurs on television. I knew I wanted to embark on the journey, and I knew what I wanted out of the destination. What I wasn't sure of was what to expect on the journey, but I did what I always did, and I established a system and a set of rules for the journey. Those rules fared well for me while I followed them, it wasn't until I started to ease off of them and break them that things began to slowly unravel.

I always kept my eye on the prize at work and in my personal life. I knew I might find a few close associates along the way, but the goal of work was to be the best I could be and show that I was the girl that anyone would want on their team, not to make friends. The goal was to be that girl, the boss chick! I had friends and could enjoy the "fun" part of life outside of work. Not that I had many friends, but the few good friends I had from college, my brother, and my husband – I knew would be there for life. Work was to professionally show my talents. I was friendly, cordial, and engaged in the banter but my life outside of work was my life and I'd determined that it was no one's business. I'd learned through the years that trust needed to be earned.

Rule #1: Work is for work, keep everything else separate.

One of my peers (a white man) always said he extended trust to everyone until they showed him, they didn't deserve it. Maybe that worked for him as a white man, but as a Black woman I'd learned the opposite. The world didn't work that way for me. I'd also learned that people utilize things they learn about you personally against you. My parents taught me, "if you get one or two good friends in your lifetime, consider yourself blessed." Because I'd learned that lesson and struggled to maintain many relationships, specifically with women along the way, I held on to that rule as the very first rule of engagement in my professional life. **Work is for work, keep everything else separate.**

Rule #2: Be a servant leader.

I sought to be a servant leader. As I knew I wanted to climb the corporate ladder and knew that I would be leading people, I wanted to be the type of leader that I'd often not had or not seen. More than that though, I wanted to be the type of leader I'd seen my dad be in the pulpit, and the type of leader I'd seen my mom be even when not holding the title of leader but being a leader in all parts of her life. I wanted to serve the people I led. I wanted to be an example and live by how I'd been raised as a Christian. I wanted people to see me and know that you could have it all, without being a snake or conniving. I wanted people to know they could be a Christian, have a family, climb the corporate ladder, and serve people in the best way. I wanted to make sure that I kept the focus on my team, their development and their success – while I trusted in God for mine. **Be a Servant Leader.**

Rule #3: You know you're a leader when the atmosphere shifts. If it doesn't shift, you aren't the leader, so you need to work at being the leader.

I was always the consummate professional. I knew that I had to remain the ultimate professional for two reasons. First, as a Black woman it was drilled into me that I needed to be twice as good to go half as far. Since I had the dreams of going to the top I knew I had a lot of work ahead of me and couldn't afford to slip in my professionalism. Second, my grandfather taught his daughters, and therefore by way of my mother— me— when a lady walks into the room, the atmosphere should shift. I believed that wholeheartedly, and also believed that when a leader walked into the room the atmosphere should shift. People should know who's the leader of the room. They should respect that leader enough to make sure any antics stopped, and I prided myself on being that person. I knew that when I walked in the room, all eyes were on me, not for the reasons I wanted, but because as a Black woman they were often waiting on a stereotype or wanting me to fail. I learned to be good with that, enjoyed it actually. I proudly proclaimed that, "I know they are looking, so they won't catch me slipping."

I enjoyed being "that girl." As I stated before, I knew that folks were looking. I knew that when I walked in rooms, I would often be the only woman, the only Black woman, or the only Black person. I knew that all eyes would be on me and that I would likely often be expected to fail or solidify what many people saw as a monolithic existence of Black women. Knowing that, I stayed on my 'A' game. I wanted people to know that when you came my way, you were going to get nothing but the best. I was determined to show up and show out in every single situation I was placed in. **You know you're a leader when the atmosphere shifts. If it doesn't shift, you aren't the leader so you need to work at being the leader.**

Rule #4: Be who you were born to be.

I never wanted to be the girl that hid her blackness. I know what you're thinking, you can't hide it. Nope, I can't hide my skin, but I could try to hide the culture part of being a Black girl from Detroit and that I wasn't willing to do. I never wanted to be the girl that hid the fact that she came from humble beginnings. I didn't want to use it as a crutch, but I'd never wanted to hide or forget it. I never wanted to forget that my work was what I do, not who I am. I would present anything I needed to do or say very professionally, but it would be me. I wouldn't change my opinions or decisions for anyone or any job. **Be who you were born to be.**

Rule #5: Everybody doesn't need to know everything.

I knew better than to ever show all of my cards. As a little girl, I remember times my dad would be heading out to take care of business and I'd say, "Daddy, can I go," and when he told me no, I'd ask, "where you goin'?" to which he'd reply, "I'm goin' to see a man 'bout a dog." I'd heard it my whole life so I knew he wasn't going to return with a dog, but that instead he meant everything was not my business and not everything would be shared with me, including where he was going. By watching Daddy and the way he operated, I realized that no one needed to know everything about me. I kept many things close to my heart and revealed them strategically only if necessary. These were things that were my business and my business only. If they weren't required to do the job, I didn't reveal them. This way of functioning also led people to confide in me. People knew that if it needed to be handled confidentially, I was the girl. My last leader often told me that. People often came to me to vent because they knew it would go no further than me. I hold things close to this day, many secrets for many people, and have no plans to reveal them, but they often helped me to strategize on how I wanted to move and choices I'd make because they helped me see how the world operates. **Everybody doesn't need to know everything.**

Rule #6: Don't put all of your eggs in one basket.

I never put all of my eggs in the same basket. Along the professional ride I'd seen organizations close-up shop with little to no warning. I'd seen people laid off, houses lost, people on the street and I didn't want that to happen to me or mine, so I always kept my options open. No matter where I was working, I kept my options open and would periodically interview. I encouraged others to do the same. I was well aware that the days of staying committed to organizations for thirty years and then being able to retire with a pension and benefits were long gone. I needed to care for myself because all businesses cared about was profits and not employees when it came down to it. I started other businesses, I attained a few degrees and certificates, and I did consulting. I just refused to only depend on one organization for my security (or at least I thought I did…more about that in future chapters). **Don't put all of your eggs in one basket.**

Rule #7: Family first, let your priorities be known.

I always made my priorities clear to anyone and everyone that may possibly have questioned or wondered what they were. There were some things that meant more to me than anything in the world and some of those things shared my last name (either the current or former last names) - they are my family, and I refused to put anything before their needs. I made it clear to any and everyone that I worked for that my family and their needs came before any job or position I may have acquired. I could get another job that I was confident of, but I could not get another family, they were all I had. I made it as easy as I could for my employers. I sat down with any calendar I had for the kids and requested time well in advance of when I needed it for events. As I climbed the ladder, I always blocked off time and scheduled meetings around things I needed to do for my family. I made sure to answer the calls of my family whenever they called. Now don't get me wrong. I'd give all I could and produce a high-quality product for everything I did, but when my family needed me, I was dropping everything. My family was my number one priority. **Family first, let your priorities be known.**

Rule #8: Document everything.

My last, but one of the most important rules was to document everything. I'd watched my mom for years keep journals. Not just journals about her feelings, but journals that included to do lists, appointments, conversations, recipes, etc. I'd seen how those journals served as records for things that may need to be recalled. So, I documented everything, I had journals for years. Over the years I had hundreds of people come through my teams and often had conversations about many things; good and bad. Since there were so many conversations, I couldn't possibly remember them all, but my documentation helped me. Years after events would take place, I'd receive calls from human resources or legal teams with questions, and I could go right to the time frame in question, and usually answer the question confidently and accurately because the journals painted very clear pictures of what was happening at any given moment. I also used my journals to help me prepare for my monthly one on ones and yearly reviews. I believed wholeheartedly that I needed to create the narrative of my career and not leave that power to anyone else. **Document everything.**

Rule #9: The New Rule – There is Power in the Pause

My rules served me well. They helped me to accomplish many things personally and professionally over the years. But I'd recently realized there was one very important rule that I'd not instituted and without it, none of the other rules mattered. I never created a rule about caring for myself. Yes, I had annual mammograms and pap smears. Yes, I'd gone to the doctor when things didn't feel quite right, but I hadn't prioritized caring for my spiritual, mental, or emotional self. I didn't even prioritize my physical self often. The one thing that I kept true to, was my every other Friday 5:30 a.m. hair appointment. Yes, I wanted my hair done, but more than that, I enjoyed the fellowship. Not many people were willing to get up at that time of morning for anything, but especially to get their hair styled or their hair cut. The patrons of the stylist and barber at "Da Shop", as the salon was called, that frequented and had standing appointments during that 5:30 a.m. -7:00 a.m. time period were all God fearing, down to earth professionals. Every other Friday morning is like a group therapy session combined with an all-out comedy show – it is healing in its own way. We all helped each other to think through situations clearly, we laughed hysterically, and I always left feeling better. That bi-weekly appointment served my need to keep my hair styled, but more than that it served a need for fellowship with like-minded people, laughter, and an acceptance of me for who I was. Being in that space helped me to start to explore all of my needs.

To be honest, I didn't even know what my needs were. I didn't realize I had unfulfilled needs, but they were now manifesting themselves through emotional and mental illnesses that had caused me to no longer be able to function in my day-to-day life. I had to take time and figure out my own needs. I felt like it was pretty sad that I didn't know my own needs, had never even thought about them, and didn't have a rule for addressing them. *How did I have a rule for everything and everybody else but ignored myself? How had I gone years and not recognized the anxiety and depression that had existed for most of my life. How had it taken me, the researcher, so long to realize that I had high functioning anxiety and depression.* I'd discovered the new rule that pulled it all together. **There is Power in the Pause**.

Chapter Ten

DELIVERING MYSELF A DOSE OF REALITY

I realized that I needed to take time to assess and analyze my own needs. In order to do that, I had to do some things I'd never done before. I had to face the truth. It had been so long since I focused on my own needs (If I'd ever focused on them), I really didn't know what they were. I needed to spend time assessing my needs and it wasn't going to be easy. It wasn't going to be easy because I didn't know how, it wasn't going to be easy because I was an expert at taking care of everyone else, not myself, and comfortable doing so, and it wasn't going to be easy because it meant everyone else had to get used to me not being their first line of defense when I hadn't taken care of myself. I needed to fill my cup to continue caring for others and pour into theirs. Up first, admitting I had an anxiety disorder and learning to manage it. I needed to be able to recognize the place I went to and the actions I took when I was experiencing anxiety.

RECOGNIZE AND MANAGE ANXIETY

Ever since my therapist diagnosed me with a severe anxiety disorder, I've been reading about anxiety. In hindsight, I realize this anxiety has been with me most of my life. I came to realize that I have what is defined as 'high-functioning anxiety.' According to the Mayo Clinic the term 'high-functioning anxiety' represents people who exhibit anxiety symptoms while maintaining a high level of functionality in various aspects of their lives. They often are successful in careers and other roles, yet internally struggle with persistent feelings of stress, self-doubt, and the fear of not measuring up. They feel extremely uncomfortable inside and struggle with significant self-criticism. To an outside observer, people with high-functioning anxiety may appear to excel and be in control. They don't appear to avoid or retreat from life. Yet behind this facade, these people have persistent thoughts of worry, fear and high-stress levels or feel on edge. When I read that definition, I realized that my picture and my life could literally replace the definition. I was always on edge, always feeling inadequate, and always feeling like something bad was bound to happen even though the facts had proven the exact opposite.

During my time away from work, I'd noticed the symptoms of anxiety I was experiencing. I also noticed how I responded during my anxiety flare ups. I recognized that I went into what I describe as hyper overdrive. I would need to be in control and do all things. I had to make sure that everything was going as I needed it to go. It caused me to create more of what I was already experiencing. I didn't have a spare moment, but I would take on more. Instead of partnering with my husband, I'd find a way to just "get it done." Instead of allowing my children to learn from their mistakes, I'd find a way to just "get it done" for them. Instead of focusing on myself and my needs, I'd find a way to just "get stuff done" by any means necessary.

My therapist diagnosed me, and I had to come with grips with it. There was a light shined on it when I had a conversation with my husband and he said to me, "babe, it is not fair for you to say you need help, you want to back away, but you keep inserting yourself." When he said that to me, I was livid. There was a situation happening with one of our children that I did not like at all. Nothing too major, just young adult stuff and watching it unfold was causing me extreme anxiety, so I went to work. I started to send emails, have conversations, make plans, and get more and more revved up. I fussed at everyone involved and was in tears about it. I was furious that he'd called me out about it and initially told him he was wrong and that I had to do things because no one else would. But that wasn't the truth, I had to do things because my anxiety told me that I had to do everything.

In order to deal with the anxiety, I realized I needed to stop in those moments and do nothing until I could think clearly. When I felt myself moving to the space of hyper overdrive, I just needed to pause and when I could think clearly, analyze the situation, assess options, and make a decision. It was hard. There were several times over the course of the leave that my therapist placed me on, I practiced pausing and doing nothing— sometimes for minutes, sometimes for months. When I got angry about things not being completed by my children, I paused and just listened. I could advise but the decision was theirs. I only had one minor, the others were grown, and they had to assess for themselves. When one of my children needed to make a major decision, I paused. When I needed to make a decision about my next steps, I paused. When I wasn't sure what to do for the day, how to feel about something, or what to say, I simply paused. I found power in the pause. Pausing gave me time to truly analyze and assess situations.

As I reflect on my life, the hyper overdrive response has always been there. I didn't see it as a response to anxiety until I started my healing journey, but that is exactly what it was. I would do things like decide I had to try to plan an entire family reunion on my own because I needed to be in control of something. When my daughter left for school, I devised a plan to buy all the things, pack the car, unpack the car, decorate the room, etc. Down to the dollar and hour. It was not just because I am an organized person, it was because I felt like I was losing control and anxiety started to set in so I grabbed hold of anything I could control and I overdid it. These events usually went something like this:

- Something happened and I felt an emotion I don't like. I either feel like I don't know how to express myself or I can't express myself in that moment.
- That "something" continues and I become a bit overwhelmed and afraid of the outcome.
- I feel myself starting to spiral—my heart rate increases, I get hot, my thoughts are racing, sometimes I can't catch my breath—anxiety has set in.
- I think, *how do I stop this? You have to get control, Ebony!*
- I find something that I can control and take control of any and everything I can, in an unreasonable way, doing everything by myself.

Let me give you an example of unreasonable. During my MBA studies, the group I was assigned was moving at a rather slow pace. All capable people, and in the end their business plan proposal project and presentation went off without a hitch. I say theirs because during one of our meetings at a small private airport, the anxiety set in and I went into overdrive, contacting my professor and telling him I would do the entire semester's work by myself if he would allow me to exit the group. I exited the group, took a week off work and spent the entire week doing the work of five people for an entire semester. Completely ridiculous I know! In the workplace, it was no different. I'd been known to put in several sixteen-hour days in a row in an effort to complete something just because I needed to be in control. In my personal life, my kids can tell you that the house became difficult to exist in when anxiety set in. No one could do anything right and everyone needed to do exactly what I said do and how I said to do it immediately. I'd somehow confused an anxiety response to simply being hardworking, organized, and a mom that was just putting her foot down.

ACCEPT AND MANAGE DEPRESSION

Depression was an altogether different beast. I needed to accept the fact that I suffered from depression and learn to manage it the same way I'd learned to manage my diabetes and got it under control. For a while I'd struggled with seasonal depressive episodes. I live in the Midwest where it is gray and dreary quite a bit. It is often cold also. I'd been here my entire life and was used to pulling myself out of a funk when the fall came. I was used to feeling the desire to run away from the snow and the cold. I was used to going to work in the dark, coming home in the dark, and only being outside on the walk to and from the car. I longed for warm nights on patios, in pools, and on beaches. I wanted a daily routine that included running outside or yoga in the park year-round. They were things I dreamed of and could experience a few months of the year and did. I understood my funk during the winter seasons. In the last few years, I came to know what I was experiencing as seasonal affective disorder and figured it was something I'd just deal with as long as I chose to live where I lived.

This depression I was currently experiencing was different. Major Depressive Disorder was different. It, too, had been around for quite some time undiagnosed. It wasn't just because it was dreary outside. It wasn't because it was cold and it wasn't coupled with a longing to just get out in the sun. This was different. I'd learned that this was not just tied to my mental and emotional state but was also chemical. This depression manifested itself in several ways. I cried constantly. I had extreme difficulty getting out of bed in the morning and sometimes at all. I continually snapped at those I loved most, and I didn't sleep well if at all. I was a mess physically. At one point, I was on five different pills, had an HbA1c of 10.7, a blood pressure that was 147/92, and I weighed close to 200 pounds. Now don't get me wrong, I know that these are issues that many people deal with, and in more severe ways, but I also know that much of it for me was related to stress, anxiety, depression, and the hormones associated with those conditions. I also experienced unexplained body aches and extreme fatigue.

I learned that this depression was not just sadness. It was chemical and I needed to do things to take control of it. I needed to recognize that just like my physical ailments, this ailment could be managed through prayer, work with my therapist and doctors, and perhaps with medication.

While I still had goals and aspirations of being the best, I no longer wanted that to be the mask by which I held in my true feelings. I wanted to be better, needed to be better, and would do it without the crutch of working daily. I learned that by working with my therapist to understand what triggered my anxiety and how I responded to it, I could deploy methods of de-escalating. I learned that anxiety didn't always look like people think, it isn't always paralyzing fear, sometimes it shows up as extreme control and the need to react in a "I can and will get it all done" type of way. I'd learned that what I was now learning to control is something that had probably been with me all my life. I'd learned to recognize when I saw this same type of anxiety in others and offered help when I could. I learned that life could not be lived without intentional pauses. By working with my care team, I also learned how to care for my depression.

By simply pausing to care for myself mentally and emotionally, I experienced a physical transformation that was amazing. My HbA1c was down to 5.4, my blood pressure was down to 112/69, I was under 170 pounds, and the energy was coming back. I was no longer yelling for the sake of yelling. I didn't cry daily. I was smiling more and just enjoying life. There was power in this pause.

I'd discovered power in this pause and wish I'd discovered it sooner. One day, my husband sent me a clip of a new podcast. A friend of a friend was doing the podcast. He shared it in hopes that I'd reach out to her and have a conversation about what she was talking about. She spoke about exactly what I was experiencing. She'd walked away from her job for what she described as "a gap year." She'd discovered the power in the pause as well.

I remember working on my dissertation and my dissertation chair telling me that I had to be finished by a certain date because the department required that she take a sabbatical every five years. I remember her telling me that the school required that she pull away from her research and teaching to rest. After her sabbatical, she would return to the school to continue teaching and doing her research but was rested and in a better mindset. The university had discovered the power of the pause.

The definition of pause is to temporarily interrupt an action or operation. When I think of the word pause, I think of hitting the pause button on a movie, a song, or a YouTube video. I am reminded of my younger years when I'd sit next to the boom box with the pause button depressed awaiting certain songs to make a mixtape or a smooth grooves tape and dubbing it with the dual cassette function. I utilized the pause button to make sure to edit out the radio DJ's voice as he announced the song. I think of the PTA acronym that is often utilized in the corporate environment—Pause Think Act. I think of pausing to gather my thoughts when making a point. When I think of pausing, I never used to think about my career, my day-to-day life, or my future. However, my current pause has caused me to think about pause in a completely different way.

I thank God for his intervention and use of my therapist to force a pause, the interactions I've had during the pause that have caused me to reconsider my meaning of pause and how to utilize it in my life. A pause that caused me to literally interrupt every action in my life for a few months. At almost fifty-years-old, I'd never hit the pause button the way I needed to. I'd been running and running and running. I'd been doing all the things that the world told me that I needed to do to be a good girl, to build a great life for me and my family, and to be a productive member of society. Unfortunately, I'd never paused to wait on the right song for me on the mixtape of my life. I'd never paused to edit out the DJ's voice. I'd not exercised PTA in the grand plan of my life. Yes, I had thought about goals, but I thought about them from the perspective of what the world said was good and what a girl like me should be doing. But the power in this pause had unleashed a part of me that I'd fallen in love with and wanted to explore. I knew this meant I had to make other really big, really serious, really difficult decisions.

The power of this pause showed me my own superpowers. I was a strategist that wanted to utilize that gift God gave me to help women like me achieve their goals, whatever they are. I loved to mentor and coach, women specifically— Black women. I loved to be a part of their journeys and celebrate their wins with them. I loved the feeling of creating something from nothing, that was the entrepreneurial bug in me that had been squished for far too long. I had friendships that had suffered for years because I didn't have the time to put into them. My children had shared their mother for sixty to seventy hours a week for their entire lives. My husband often got the tired, unenthusiastic, frustrated, agitated part of me that was left after I'd given all to the good things I had to offer in spaces that meant the least to me. It was time for all of that to change. I needed to push into the things that I loved, I needed to give all of me to the people I loved, and I needed to be healthy—spiritually, physically, emotionally, and most of all mentally.

Chapter Eleven

WE ALL HAVE CHOICES

My first attempt at attending college didn't end well. I was out in the big bad world on my own for the first time and it chewed me up and spit me out multiple times. I trusted people I should not have trusted, and it made it hard for me to focus when I found out they did not mean the naïve seventeen-year-old any good at all. I thought I'd found love when I had not – let's just say that ended badly. All in all, I just made some really bad choices. I missed the comfort, security, and safety of home once I came to my senses, so I transferred schools and gave it a second try. Making that move was one of the best decisions I have ever made. I met my very best friend and had a blast for the rest of my undergraduate career. When I first transferred to the school, I was placed on a co-ed floor. On this floor is where I met my best friend. I also met a group of the coolest guys you ever want to meet. Being that we were at a small predominately white institution just north of our hometown of Detroit, most of the Black people that attended were from Detroit, and there was a connection and energy among the Black students that created a special bond. We understood each other's backgrounds and cheered for each other's futures.

As we went about the normal days of college students, attending classes together, going to parties, playing spades in the lounge, pledging, or supporting those that were pledging, and playing harmless pranks on each other, there were a number of sayings that we adopted or coined. One of those sayings was "we all got choices." I was reminded of that saying, those times, and those people at this time in my life.

Boy did I have choices to make. Major choices. As a college undergraduate, choices were just as difficult for that time in my life. But I had a circle of friends that would support me and even if I made the wrong choice, redemption and rebounding was inevitable as we were determined to see each other succeed. So, when I failed the Calculus 2 exam and burst into uncontrollable tears that made one of those really cool male friends of mine feel immensely uncomfortable, he still comforted me through his discomfort and told me we would figure it out. I eventually changed my major from engineering and have done quite well in the business world and he is now finishing a PhD in mathematics, so while it didn't look the way we thought it would, he was in fact correct...we figured it out. When I decided to change my major, the dean of the school of engineering reminded me that as the president of the school's chapter of the National Society of Black Engineers the students of color needed me as an example. I reminded him that I could still be that example of a leader but one that didn't forget about their own needs. I was reelected as a business major for a second term as president and did just what I said. I remained an example of a leader to the students of color and attended to my needs in the process. When I chose to apply and become a Resident Assistant, it was simply to cover my room and board nothing more, but it put me in front of several underclassmen that I became a friend to or mentored. Years later when having lunch with one of those friends, she revealed that she always admired me and looked to do many of the things that I had done because she saw me do them…I was blown away because I was always impressed by her and had no idea she was watching me. So yes, I had choices to make, but I've always had choices to make. I could use these real-life experiences to help me make the choices I needed to make now.

Decision #1, I needed to decide whether or not I was going to take medication for depression. While I still had my best friend at my side and thank God, she is a practicing psychologist that could give me advice as a friend, but also as a professional, I didn't have that cool group of guys down the hall. Thirty years later, we were all still in touch through social media and in some cases in person, but we were in different phases of our lives so I couldn't just blurt out a problem over a game of spades and expect it to be solved or burst into tears uncontrollably and expect that in a few hours we'd go to the frat, sorority, or Black Student Union Party for the week and it would all work itself out. But what I did have now was a hell of a support system that no matter the decision I made would be there for me.

Medicine has always concerned me. Anyone that knows me will tell you that I will tough out pain before even taking a Motrin. Maybe it is because taking medicine has always had extreme effects on me. When most people can pop a pain killer for a headache and go about their day, I can take the same pill and need to sleep for hours, not be able to drive, and will feel drugged for much of the day. Maybe it was because I'd grown up in the 80s in the midst of the "war on drugs" and saw both legal and illegal drugs ruin lives and entire families, many of which would never recover. Maybe it is because I have a very addictive personality and I didn't want to become addicted to anything that was bad for me. Maybe it was because I genuinely believed that God provided all the medicine we needed in plants, we just had to discover the correct mix to make it effective. Whatever the reason, I had a real concern, especially when it came to taking medication that could impact my brain's chemistry.

I realized I needed to take the emotion out of it and lean into my researcher and strategist strong suits to determine what to do. I first needed to research the class of medications being suggested. The research would need to include the opinions of my therapist, my MD, my husband, and my best friend, but also, I had to read. After much research and prayer, I decided to pause for a bit. When I finally worked up the nerve to take the medication, the first medication that was prescribed didn't go well. I don't know if it was all in my head or not, but I felt like my entire pelvic region was going numb. The doctor prescribed an alternative and it sat on my kitchen counter for two weeks. As I walked past it daily, it was almost as if I was having a conversation with it. *Should I really take you? Are you going to be with me forever if I do? Are you going to have side effects? Can I get better without taking you?* I felt like the medication was taunting me. In the end, I decided to take the medication because I wanted…I needed to be better.

Decision #2, I needed to decide whether to leave my job and career that I worked so hard on behind. It was not an easy decision but after much deliberation and prayer I knew that I needed to leave my job to explore the part of me that I'd recently fallen in love with, but more than that, I needed to leave the job to be a healthier me. I was leaving the stress of doing things that I was good at just for a paycheck. It was not healthy for me or any of the relationships in my life. I'd realized that my job and the stress created by not doing what I was put here to do, were causing irreparable damage to my physical, mental, and emotional life. I want to set the record straight by saying that I worked with amazing people who were loving, kind, caring, and extremely talented. The company that I worked for paid well, had excellent benefits, and in my opinion did its best to treat its employees well. The problem was that I didn't care about 90% of the things I had to do daily and the things I enjoyed the most were not being developed or allowed to shine, they were being suffocated. What I did daily was no longer in line with my dreams and desires. I'd developed and matured as a woman, a professional, and an entrepreneur and had reached the goals I set as a young woman, so now I had new desires. Also, as I'd grown in my faith, there were just some things that now troubled my spirit, and I could no longer turn a blind eye to (nothing wrong by the world's standards or illegal – just not in alignment with who I am).

After much prayer and deliberation, I also decided to leave my job. I wanted to use the gifts God gave me in a different way. I'd be lying if I said that I heard the audible voice of God tell me to leave my job because I did not, but I do believe I felt in my spirit that it was time. I had no idea why I felt that God chose this time for me to leave. What I did know was that it felt right. I had to make amends with the guilt I felt for leaving and know that the plans God had for me were for me. I had to remind myself in the several months that I was away from the job, the company did not miss a beat, nor did any of my teams or team members. What God had for them was for them, too.

Let me be 100% clear. I am not recommending that everyone reading this book experiencing a similar crisis to what I experienced leave their job. That is not feasible for everyone, and I would not suggest that blindly. My circumstances are different than yours and you have to make the decision that is right for you. What I am suggesting is that you find a way to move away from stress into peace. I am suggesting that you find a way to pause to make a clear decision. I am suggesting that you understand your current situation and make a move toward a future that allows you total healing. I am suggesting you find a way to quiet the noise and hear from God.

Before the final decision was made, my therapist suggested a 2nd extension. Along with my doctor they believed that a second extension would be most beneficial and help me make the clearest decision possible. The company honored the leave, but the disability company, that is an entirely different beast. After two denials and an appeal, the final decision of Lincoln Financial was that I needed "exposure therapy." I needed to get out of the house and be exposed to work. It is almost laughable that a white man who had no idea who I was or what I was experiencing made that decision based on a five-question survey asked of me on one day. My entire medical crisis was being dismissed and they denied twelve weeks of pay for my leave. I share this because I want anyone reading to know that stopping to take care of your mental health will be supported outwardly by all and behind closed doors by some, but for some (even those in the profession) – they will only provide performative support and when the rubber meets the road, they will take the other side, so be prepared for an additional fight. As you fight for your mental health, you may have to fight for your pay, or fight a doctor, or fight for care – this fight is not for the faint at heart, which is the exact opposite of what anyone needs when experiencing this type of crisis.

Decision #3 was probably the hardest, because it is still not complete. It will probably change several times before I settle into a routine. I had to decide how to make money going forward. What would life look like for me as a career woman? I had a grand vision, but I know making it true takes strategy, planning, resources and above all – prayer. While I wished that I was independently wealthy, I was not, so I had to do something to continue to make income. I had to figure out how to continue to contribute to the lifestyle that we'd built as a family. I knew it wouldn't be easy, but I knew that God would provide, so I went into prayer about it and luckily with God's help, we are making it work.

Many people, including me, will tell you to just take the first step. That I did, but being the planner and strategist that I am and not wanting to trigger my anxiety more than what might naturally be triggered just by the day-to-day ups and downs of being an entrepreneur, I decided not to forge ahead on this journey alone. I hired people to help me. I settled on six streams that that I knew I would be good at. I prioritized the streams based on what I believed was my spirit leading me, and I went to work on researching people that were good at those things and hired them to help me not only learn from their mistakes but build business around the streams. Being good at something is one thing, but building a business around it is something completely different.

It felt good to be doing work for myself. It felt good to know that the work I was doing was helping others in a way that my previous work had not. It felt good to know that I was taking a chance on me, but this me was different. This me was healing and working on being a better me, so what the world got was the better me. It felt good to take care of me.

Chapter Twelve

THE PAUSE FRAMEWORK

As mentioned earlier, it wasn't easy doing the work to get better. It required that I reflected on many hurtful things that happened to me during my life, but it also required that I celebrate the many triumphs and accomplishments. As a researcher and lifelong learner at heart, I often find myself coding things in my mind, making categories, looking for similarities, and trying to find patterns. When reflecting on my life, I realized that I of course followed my rules, but I also followed a framework that helped me to manage the most difficult times and allowed me to make the most difficult decisions. This framework sometimes only took a few hours and sometimes it took months, like you read about in the previous chapters, but each time it worked. It is the Power of the PAUSE. Let me be clear, this framework is not a replacement for therapy or for medication when it is needed, but it is a system that can help you through difficult times and difficult decisions. Again, it is NOT a replacement for therapy, medication or prayer – it is a supplement to those things.

Step 1: Pause and Pray- Literally, pause and pray. You have to stop what you are doing and do nothing for a bit. I know that pausing is sometimes not as easy as it seems, but everything doesn't have to be done right now. You have to stop. If you need to make a big decision, if you find yourself spiraling out of control, if you just can't think straight—pause. Don't do anything, consider taking a day off if you can, a quick staycation may be the answer, or like I did many evenings, just sit in your car, in your closet, or anywhere you can get a little peace of mind. Then pray! And I mean pray for real. I am not a theologian, and believe me, I am not trying to get you to believe what I believe. What you believe is a personal decision. The only people I don't understand are those that don't believe in any higher power, but that is a conversation for a different day. I believe that Jesus Christ is my savior, and so when I pray, I pray to God in the name of Jesus. I encourage you to do the same - pray! Pray a real prayer, it doesn't have to be fancy, but it has to be sincere. I believe that God wants to hear the earnest requests of our hearts. Pray out loud, let the tears run if they need to, just pray.

By pausing and praying, you give yourself permission to take off the cape. You give yourself permission to step out of the limelight. You give yourself permission to be transparent and vulnerable. I believe God will hear the desires of your heart. In that prayer ask that God provide you clarity and help you move forward in or from your current circumstances. Ask that He help you learn the lessons and do the work to continue to grow and I believe He will do just that as you follow the next steps. I believe He will give you peace on the path that He has for you. You have to pause though to even get there.

Step 2: Assess, Analyze, and Articulate- This step helps you get what is in your head out of your head and make sense of it. I typically achieve this step through writing, although there are other means of accomplishing this goal. In this step, you must honestly ask yourself questions to help you assess where you are. Then you must analyze how you got there. After you have figured that out, you have to find a way to articulate it.

The reason it is important for you to go through this step is because it helps you hold a mirror to yourself. This is not about looking outwardly but turning your focus inward. In the most cases, there is something we have done to contribute to our current circumstances. Whether it is making a bad decision or simply making no decision at all, we have some part in our current circumstances and asking questions directed at oneself will help to assess and analyze our part in it. I personally don't believe you have completed this step until you can clearly articulate your part in whatever situation or circumstance you find yourself needing to pause from.

Step 3: Understanding- Once you have clearly articulated your role in your current circumstance, you can start to understand deeply. Not only understand how you got there - maybe it isn't the first time so you are now noticing habits, but you can also start to understand why you don't want to be there any longer. You can begin to understand where you would like to be instead. A full understanding is needed to move to a better experience. Once you have a full understanding of the "how" you got there, "why" you don't want to be there, and "where" you want to be instead you can move to the next step.

Step 4: Strategize, Set Goals, and Plan- Now it is time to make some moves. It is time to strategize, set goals, and create a plan. Now this may seem very corporate, but it works for me in my personal life. I remember my mom telling me, "If more people spent as much time planning their marriage as they did their weddings, maybe more marriages would last." I believe that to be the case as we move through life. If we want to have different results, we have to do something different, but we can't just do it on a whim. It takes thought and intention to develop and become better than the person you were the day before. Strategize, set goals, and plan. I also believe you have to leave room for "divine disruption" along the way.

Step 5: Execute and Evaluate- Once you have written the vision and made it plain through step four it is now time to put the plan into action. You have to do what you wrote. You must find the discipline to do what you planned. If your plan is like mine and requires that you shut your mouth at times, you have to find the discipline to do that. Believe me when I tell you, you won't get it right, right out the gate and you won't do right every time, but with discipline and determination things will change. Just keep executing then take time to evaluate. Are you doing a good job? Did you make the right plan? How can you get better? When you ask these questions, one of two things is going to happen—you will determine that you nailed it, and you are good to go or you will determine that you need to start the pause framework over because you have some more work to do.

When I look back over my life, I realize that every time I was able to pull myself out of a bad situation or circumstance this is how I did it. Not all situations were bad on the outside, but somewhere bad for me internally. When I realized I was operating well below my potential in high school and wanted to do better, I P.A.U.S.E.d and was able to excel. When I realized I was at the wrong college, with the wrong people, doing the wrong things, I P.A.U.S.E.d and got back on track at a new university. When I looked around and realized that I didn't want to graduate in the summer but I wanted to be a part of the main graduation during the spring and my parents deserved that as well, I P.A.U.S.E.d, determined that God would see me through the seemingly impossible (working full time and taking eighteen credits) to make it happen. When I was a year into my marriage and thought it was failing, I P.A.U.S.E.d with my husband and now twenty-two years later we are still in this thing together. When the engine went out in one car, the transmission in the other and we had two toddlers to transport and jobs to get to, I P.A.U.S.E.d and we never missed a day of work and the kids got to where they needed to go. It is only when I don't P.A.U.S.E. that things seem to go worse. I have discovered the power in the P.A.U.S.E. and I hope you do as well.

Bonus Chapter

HIT RECORD, LEAVING A LEGACY

My life after the pause is bound to be completely different. Life is easier in some ways and more challenging in others. I now wear multiple hats that require balance in a very different way than what a 9 to 5 (more like 8 to 7) required. I have to have discipline that no one will hold me accountable for, if I don't hold myself accountable. The check is not just deposited, I have to go out and get it. I have to be an extreme strategist, planner, and entrepreneur. But I get to do the things I've always enjoyed and have a passion for. I get to write daily and speak about things I am passionate about. I get to coach people to achieve their dreams. I get to build businesses and leave a legacy. I get to be a present mom and wife and happy human. I know that my anxiety has to continue to be managed. I now see the signs and simply P.A.U.S.E. I spend more time in therapy and am better able to manage the anxiety that I feel less and less these days. I know that depression may return and understand that it is an illness like any other that requires that I treat it when it arises through talk therapy and sometimes medication. Burnout is no longer an option for me. I know what contributed to the burnout and now refuse to let it happen again—the world has to get Ebony, all of Ebony—raw and unfiltered, and I now teach others to do the same. I continue to focus on pausing when necessary.

I get to be a writer. I get to write blog posts, articles, books, and create content to help other women build their dream lives and learn from the lessons of my life. Writing has always been a part of my life and has been healing for me. As an introvert it allows me to get things out of my mind and heart that are sometimes difficult to verbalize. When I was working for others, I was able to write a few things, and even acted as a ghostwriter for things that my leaders needed to write and publish, but I didn't get to fully explore the talent God blessed me with. Even in school, I had to write about what others thought I should be writing about. But now, I get to write about what makes me happy. I've been told that my writing style is unique and relatable, and I hope it is. For the most part, my writing is simply my inner thoughts, but now I get to utilize my inner thoughts and joy in writing as a part of my day-to-day life and career. I'm even exploring some ghost-writing opportunities.

I also get to speak and tell my story. As a young girl, I was often frightened to speak in front of people. I skipped speech class and any class that required public speaking so I wouldn't have to be embarrassed. My self-confidence was low and even though I'd pace back and forth in my room delivering speeches to a mirror that I wished I could deliver to groups of people, I couldn't find the confidence to do it at that age. In college, I pushed myself to take a speech class again and wrote and delivered speeches through extreme fear and trembling. Those speeches became a powerful force to show me that I could work through my fear and could accomplish things despite negative inner voices. I branched out and gave speeches to run for office in student organizations. I practiced and I practiced and eventually got to a place where I became energized when I got a mic in my hand. I became comfortable delivering speeches in front of hundreds and sometimes thousands in my corporate career. Now I get to tell my story to help others on different stages.

I studied mentorship during my doctoral studies and absolutely love it. I still have a special place in my heart for mentoring young women looking to figure out the direction they'd like to go. I get to run a program that teaches young Christian women how to navigate this crazy world as they grow in age and in their faith. I also get to coach professionals that are well on their chosen paths. I get to help them get there and excel once there. I get to work with the most amazing women as they design lives that make them smile, provide the desires of their heart, and live lives that they have designed instead of lives that someone else has designed for them.

I get to express my creativity through my entrepreneurial ventures. I get to build with my own hands. I get to show up as a partner for my husband in a whole different way. I get to make sure that the fruits of my labor are benefiting my community. I get to reap the entirety of the rewards of my hard work and suffer the consequences when wrong decisions are made. I get to show my children what it means to sacrifice for long term goals and push into your purpose for life and enjoy your work. I get to leave a legacy for my family.

Lastly, but most importantly, I get to be the wife and mom that I want to be. I get to cook the dinners I want regularly. I get to stop in the middle of the day and run the errand that my husband needs me to run. I get to redecorate the house. I get to take the bowling balls to my son that he forgot in the morning – better yet, I get to watch his matches during the week without asking permission. I get to accompany my daughter on her photoshoot on a Tuesday as she starts her entrepreneurial journey without trying to see if I have enough PTO for that and all the other things happening this year. I get to be a happy and fulfilled human.

I took some time to reflect not only on this experience, but my life in general. I realized that even though I may have struggled most of my life with some form and some degree of anxiety and/or depression, it had to be God's plan for me to go through part of my life that way so that I could be a living testimony and help others that suffer in the same way. I am of the belief that God allowed the journey as it was so that this book could be written. I believe that the journey had to happen just as it did for the next leg of the journey to work the way God intended.

In the process, I inadvertently created a framework. The P.A.U.S.E framework that I utilize to help women in the workplace achieve their goals through thoughtful reflection, strategic planning, and extreme execution and of course prayer. The P.A.U.S.E framework is a framework that assisted me during some really rough times. I realized that this framework could help me move forward in a different way, now that I was aware of it. Sometimes it took me a short amount of time to work through the framework and sometimes it was a lot longer, like this current pause. Sometimes the pause needed to be extreme and sometimes it needed to be quick, but it always worked and this time it had worked in a major way. It helped me tremendously and I am sure that it was going to continue to help me in the future. My family, coaching clients, workshop participants, and conference attendees get the full benefit of the P.A.U.S.E.

NOTE TO READERS

Hello trailblazer:

If you made it this far in this book, I want to thank you for hanging out with me as I talked through my entire journey. If you are still here, chances are you are experiencing something similar or have at some point in your lifetime. To the outside world, you are taking life by the horns and killing it. People admire you; you are an example for others to follow, and quite frankly, you are proud of yourself and all that you have accomplished. However, you are probably tired, starting to question the journey you are on and if it is the journey you really want to be on, and you may also be dealing with some emotional and mental health issues like me. My guess is that these reasons (and maybe a few more) have caused you to continue to read to the end.

If you are anything like me, you want the conversation to continue. I get really connected to characters in books or on television shows. When I read memoirs, I often start researching to find out what the person is doing now and how life has changed if at all for them. I start to wonder who else has the same thoughts, curiosities, and questions about the subject as me. Knowing how I feel, I am hoping I am right to guess that the readers of this book feel the same. So, I have created spaces to continue the conversation of what it feels like to be a Black woman on a career journey, reaching the highest heights, sometimes experiencing burnout, and wanting to connect with like-minded women that can support you through these times and on your journey.

Join the trailblazer community and continuing the conversation by subscribing on my website www.drebonystone.com. You can also join the conversation on LinkedIn https://www.linkedin.com/in/drebonystone/, or on Instagram https://www.instagram.com/dr.ebonystone.com/ . By joining me and the rest of the community on one or all of these platforms, you will be able to continue the conversation, engage with women just like you, experiencing similar journeys, and get answers to questions that are seemingly the most difficult. Please feel free to grab your copy of the P.A.U.S.E journal to help you practice pausing and reflecting. This journal is full of weekly writing prompts to help you reflect, release, and remind you of the Power of the Pause. You can download a copy at www.drebonystone.com/pause-journal. Thank you for reading and I will see you in the virtual world soon.

Ebony Stone

P.S. Keep your eyes open for the prequel to this book, and the sequel.

DISCUSSION QUESTIONS

1. Ebony talks about creating an alter ego (She) or wearing a mask that doesn't allow others to experience her fully. Many call that code switching in the corporate environment. Would you describe Ebony's experiences throughout life as code switching, why or why not? How have you experienced code switching in your life?

2. Ebony describes multiple situations in which she had difficulties building genuine, lasting relationships with other black women despite their commonalities. This is also something commonly spoken about among black women. Why does this phenomenon exist and how can we work to eliminate it?

3. Have you ever had the feeling of not being able to escape and finding refuge in bathrooms, closets, or in cars like Ebony? What led to the feeling of not being able to escape?

4. Where do we draw the line between sacrifice for those we care most for (spouse, children, parents, etc.) and caring for self?

5. Ebony describes an incident at work after the George Floyd murder where she was a willing participant in eliminating her own safe space and ability to process her own grief. She felt responsible to provide clarity around her feelings so others

understood instead of fully processing. Discuss why that feeling of responsibility exists and if you've experienced it?

6. Discuss the performative acceptance of anxiety, depression, and other mental illnesses that is coupled with the lack of full acceptance as evidenced through the insurance company's rejection of Ebony's claim.

7. Why is there an overall reluctance of people to share their battles with mental illness or even classify what they are dealing with as mental illness.

8. Discuss the indirect impact of the unmanaged anxiety and or depression on the loved ones of the person experiencing the condition.

9. As therapy becomes more and more accepted as a part of the caring for one's self, should it be a part of preventative regimens like physicals and dental cleanings? Why or why not?

10. Do you have your own set of rules that you live by? Are those rules different inside and outside of work?

11. What element(s) of the P.A.U.S.E. framework do you think we as black women are the best/worst at executing. Which one(s) are you best or worst at?

12. Did you enjoy reading this book and would you recommend it to others?

RESOURCES

1. Therapy for Black Girls – www.therapyforblackgirls.com
2. The Black Mental Health Alliance – www.blackmentalhealth.com
3. The Boris L. Henson Foundation – www.borislhensonfoundation.org
4. The National Alliance on Mental Illness – www.nami.org
5. Black Female Therapist – www.blackfemaletherapist.org
6. U.S. Department of Labor – Family Medical Leave Act - Family and Medical Leave Act | U.S. Department of Labor (dol.gov)
7. Unveiling the Silent Struggle: Black Women and Anxiety - Black Women and Anxiety | Spelman College
8. Anxiety & Depression Association of America – www.adaa.org
9. National Institute of Health – www.nih.org
10. Very Well Mind – www.verywellmind.com
11. Psychology Today – www.psychologytoday.com

Made in the USA
Columbia, SC
23 December 2024

50544930R00090